THE MISSIONARY
AND HIS CRITICS

THE MISSIONARY
AND HIS CRITICS

REV. JAMES L. BARTON

Young People's Missionary Movement of the
United States and Canada

THE MISSIONARY AND HIS CRITICS

BY
REV. JAMES L. *Levi* BARTON

43864

THIRD EDITION

New York: 158 Fifth Avenue
Chicago: 80 Wabash Avenue
Toronto: 25 Richmond St., W.
London: 21 Paternoster Square
Edinburgh: 100 Princes Street

Foreword

THIS little book does not pretend to be a scientific treatise on missions or missionaries. It is merely an attempt to present some of the simple facts of foreign missionary operations in common every day language without officialism or cant. To this is added the testimony of men, the most of whom have an international reputation and who, after personal inspection, speak of what they have seen and know to be true. These are disinterested and unprejudiced witnesses whose testimony would convince any fair-minded jury or obtain a favorable verdict from the bench of any high court of the world. Whoever would unjustly criticise or maliciously sneer at foreign missionaries, must be prepared to reckon with this mass of evidence, which is but a fraction of what might easily be gathered.

I am greatly indebted to Mrs. Barton for her painstaking care in collecting and copying quotations used in this volume, and to Miss Martha T. Fiske for the comprehensive index, making the quotations easily available for all purposes.

J. L. B.

BOSTON, MASS., OCT. 17, 1906.

CONTENTS

The Missionary and His Critics

THE IDEALS OF THE MISSIONARY

The Missionary and His Critics

I

THE MERCHANT AND THE MISSIONARY

ARE missionaries forcing themselves upon an unwilling people? This is an old and frequently answered question, and yet it is ever new, judging by the number of times it is asked to-day, both by intelligent and often professing Christian people and by some of the leading secular papers. The question is asked as an implied criticism of the work of the foreign missionaries who are in countries like Turkey, India, China, and Japan. Many who have but superficial knowledge of affairs in these countries attribute some, if not all, general disturbances, like the Armenian massacres and the Boxer uprising, to the presence and work of the missionaries, and they ask, " Why are we forcing our religion upon these people? " The assumption is that if no missionaries were sent, there would be no disturbances, the people themselves would be far happier and more prosperous, and our own government would be saved a vast amount of international difficulty. The arguments offered are somewhat as follows:

1. These Oriental people are content with their ancestral religions and do not ask for ours; why, then,

do we volunteer to send them our Christianity? In the Turkish Empire the Moslems are perfectly satisfied with Islam; they have not asked for instruction in Christianity. As a race they do not desire nor as a government permit Mohammedans to embrace Christianity. The Armenian churches in Turkey were Christian long before Protestantism was named, and with that Church, the Armenians as a whole were fairly content.

In India the Mohammedans are as satisfied as are their co-religionists in Turkey, while the Hindus, before their contact with the civilized world, felt they possessed the most ancient and most complete religion in the world. They were proud of their sacred books and equally sacred traditions, and zealous for their venerable temples and forms of worship. Certainly, the 220,000,000 Hindus could not be charged with being dissatisfied with their own religion, and with asking the Western world to send them teachers to instruct them in the principles of a new faith.

There is no evidence that the 400,000,000 in China have ever expressed a desire for a religion to supersede their national faith. Ancestral worship and the moral teachings of Confucius have been regarded by them as quite ample for all their needs. There are even Chinese, not a few, who are free to declare that, after an observation of the practical operations of Christianity in so-called Christian countries, they are satisfied that China requires no new religion.

The same is said of Japan. Their religion has proved adequate to their needs for many thousand years, and they did not ask, when the country was opened to the West, that the Occident should send them its religion.

2. Moreover, these Oriental religions have proved themselves to be adapted to the methods of life and the way of thinking peculiar to the Oriental nations, whereas Christianity introduces that which is strange and even revolutionary to the Orient. Their own religions sat easily upon them and seemed to fit exactly at every point, which certainly cannot be said of the religion of Jesus Christ. The question is therefore asked, " Why should anyone wish to disturb the peace of mind of those countries, introduce discussions and even controversies, teach a religion that necessarily must make divisions in society, and, in a word, take any step that tends to de-orientalize the delightfully ancient Orient? "

3. Those who look at the matter more directly from the religious standpoint say, " There is some good in all the non-Christian religions. Why assume that the excellencies they actually contain are not sufficient for the needs of those who profess them? No one will deny that each of these old religions contains much, in its sacred books and in its traditions, that is highly commendable. Is it unreasonable to assume that these peoples are in the hands of God, and that He has made to them a sufficient revelation of divine truth? It is conceded generally that Christianity contains many moral precepts and much in the way of practical instruction for the life of the individual of which these several religions of

the East know nothing, and yet why should we assume that it is essential that they have these additional truths laid before them at all? In a word, the East has its own religion; why not leave it to work out its own salvation with the light it already possesses?"

The above declarations, or similar ones, one hears or reads, in whole or in part, almost daily, and, for many, an answer is difficult to frame.

It is not my purpose to present here a line of argument to cover in detail the objections to foreign missions implied in the above statements. My purpose is more to hold the question up for a general and wide view, that we may consider it in its broader aspects, and in due relation to some of the other large questions of our day. If friends of foreign missions are open to the charge of narrowness, I am free to say that the opponents of missions cannot always be credited with breadth of vision.

I wish to waive for the present discussion that fundamental principle of our Christian faith that makes it obligatory upon every professed follower of Jesus Christ to make His gospel known to all men and all races. "His not to reason why." Loyalty to Christ demands this, no matter what the present religion of a people is, how perfect or how defective its precepts and practices.

First, let us consider another kind of missionary work prosecuted in foreign lands and supported by funds contributed in this country. These foreign missionary operations are older than what goes by the name of "modern foreign missions," cost more, have a larger financial backing, and undoubtedly are far more popular. We hear few objections to their operations, which are aided by treaties and governments, supported by navies, and pushed with great aggressiveness. I refer to "Commercial Foreign Missions."

Let us briefly survey some of the operations of this propagandism in the countries already referred to above. By consulting the consular reports and the trade journals of this country we find that European and American manufacturers and merchants have sent commercial missionaries to all of the foreign ports and many of the interior cities of Turkey, China, India, and Japan, as well as other countries; and are now maintaining them—missionaries whose sole object and purpose is to convert the natives of those countries to a recognition of the superior value of the particular article or articles handled by the individual missionary, and to lead them to adopt the same.

The traveler in those countries finds that foreign clocks and watches have been introduced everywhere in the great centers, while through the employment of a large paid native agency the propaganda is pushed into interior districts. The plan of this movement contemplates the introducing into every home of the East a clock of some kind, as well as a watch for every person who can raise the funds to purchase it. The traveler in the East and Far East cannot fail to be impressed with the success of the efforts of these time-piece missionaries. A traveler recently visited the Imperial palace in China and saw there nearly two hundred clocks of various forms and values.

The sewing-machine missionary has penetrated all these countries. American sewing machines are operating to-day not only in the great ports of the Orient, but I have seen them in the mountains of Kurdistan, in the villages of interior India, and in the heart of China. Few commercial missionaries are more alert and aggressive than these.

The same can be said in a large measure of the missionary who represents the manufacturers of bicycles. In the earlier days, and even recently, a man upon a bicycle in parts of Turkey, India, and China, excited the people, and in cases not a few led to incipient riots. To-day in those same places the foreign wheel is almost as commonplace as the native cart or the ubiquitous donkey.

American kerosene has its missionary in those same countries, and his work, too, has not been a failure. Probably no other branch of foreign commercial missionary propagandism has more completely penetrated to the interior of the Orient, and more completely won the approval of the natives. I have seen caravan loads of these wares penetrating into the least civilized parts of the Turkish Empire, great masses of kerosene tins piled up at interior railroad stations in India; while the tin of empty American kerosene cans has become a staple article of local trade all over the East. One of the American Ministers at Constantinople told me some years ago that his principal occupation was to look after the importation of American kerosene.

Foreign food-stuff missionaries are everywhere in the East. I have seen posted along the railroads in India, advertisements of certain brands of American and European invalid and infant foods, the advertisement so worded as to attract the attention of the Hindu, declaring that it was made without the touch of the hands of the workmen.

Years ago, American flour merchants sent agents of their wares to Hong Kong, but when they attempted to trade with the Chinese they found that they all preferred their rice to Western flour. The agents did not despair. They imported thousands of dollars worth of flour, baked it into attractive forms which seemed suited to the tastes of the Chinese, and gave it away in lavish profusion. This continued for years, till an appetite for the products of foreign flour was created among the people, and then trade began. The statistics of trade with China for 1903 show that over $2,000,000 worth of American flour was imported into China in that one year. Foreign locomotives and railroad iron have been introduced into China by the agents of the manufacturers. This has required great patience and persistence, but the energy of the commercial missionaries who had the matter in charge proved to be sufficient for the occasion.

Perhaps these illustrations are sufficient for our purposes, although the list might be prolonged almost indefinitely. It is evident that manufacturing firms and merchants in Europe and the United States are sustaining in the Far East, at great cost, a large number of commercial agents or missionaries whose sole object is to open a market there for the permanent sale of the wares they represent, and to accomplish this purpose they teach the people how to use their various products, and endeavor to form in them the habit of using the same.

Now let us apply to these commercial missionaries the same criticisms or objections that have been applied above to the Christian missionary whose object is to introduce Christian principles and institutions to these same people, to see if the objections of the one do not apply with equal, if not greater, force to the other.

1. These people were content with their own local conditions and were not asking for foreign wares. Why distract them by creating a discontent? We have no evidence that the Orient, either *en masse* or as individuals, ever felt that hand sewing was not quite rapid enough to meet every need, and that the rising and the setting of the sun did not mark time with sufficient accuracy. We are well aware that China not only did not desire the locomotive or foreign railroad iron, but tore up the first railroad and destroyed the engines. What Oriental ever expressed, of his own initiative, a desire for Western flour; or is it known that an individual ever, of his own volition, was dissatisfied with the illuminating facilities of his country, and desired foreign lamps and oil?

2. The original condition of these Oriental peoples well met their desires and ambitions, while the introduction of foreign wares changed their conditions and created new desires. Society was such that there was no need or wish for a close and accurate measurement of time. The division into years, moons, days, and morning and night, was ample. The leisure of the people was so great, and their need of elaborate garments so slight, that hand sewing met every requirement without a thought of hardship or a desire for a change. To peoples who retired for the most part soon after sunset, or gathered into groups for gossip, the simple native oil lamps were amply sufficient, in their own judgment. And for purposes of travel, the house-boat, the caravan, and the ox-cart, which had met the needs of the fathers to the hundredth generation in the past, were sufficient in every particular, in the judgment of the people, for their own needs. They did not demand or desire the bicycle or the railroad.

As these foreign products and inventions came in, they began at once to change the customs of life of the people. Oriental exclusiveness, content, and calm were broken in upon, and, in multitudes of cases, disturbances were created by the new order of things. They were content with the original conditions; why disturb and distract them with new and undemanded wares?

3. Their old customs had some good in them; why assume that the new order is better? No one can live for any length of time in the East and not be im-

pressed with the fact that the simplicity of Oriental customs and society has much that is commendable. The repose that characterizes it, the absence of worry and rush, the assurance that what was good enough for the fathers is good enough for the sons, are delightfully refreshing to one who is familiar with the feverish haste of our own land, and the constant struggle for new methods.

Why should our commercial missionaries assume that what they are offering is better for the Orientals than that which they already possess? Is it not reasonable to assume that the good in what the Orientals have is amply good enough for them, although it would not be good enough for us?

I submit that every one of these arguments against the acts of the commercial missionary is just as valid as when used against the Christian missionary. Do not let it be understood that I am opposed to the external advancement of the Oriental races. I would not be engaged in the foreign missionary work if I were. Religious advancement always implies social and commercial enlargement. The educated and Christianized Oriental will always welcome the Occidental merchant as he welcomes the Christian teacher from the West. The man who argues thus against the foreign Christian missionary uses arguments that, with equal force, would keep out the merchant and the agent of foreign manufacturing firms.

Let us go one step further. The merchant enters the Orient largely for selfish reasons. He has, ordinarily, no interest in the advancement and material welfare of the Oriental. He desires only to sell goods and make a profit from such sales. He is trying to establish an Oriental trade for what he can make out of it. The goods he sells may be most harmful to the purchaser, or they may be a real blessing. That makes no particular difference to him, and does not enter into his plans in pushing trade. This enterprise, while selfish in its plans and purposes, has the general approval of the Western public, and is backed by all the machinery of government. The outraged merchant in foreign countries demands and rightfully obtains diplomatic support, and, if need be, the navy is sent for his protection. Senator Lodge of Massachusetts said not long since, " We believe in trade expansion. By every legitimate measure within the province of government and the Constitution we mean to stimulate the expansion of our trade and open new markets." This imposing, at times by force, of foreign products upon the Oriental peoples, is solely for the purposes of private gain.

On the other hand, the Christian foreign missionary is in the Orient purely and solely for the good of the people. He may not always be wise in his methods, but he cannot be charged with having any selfish purpose in his efforts. His teachings are never forced upon the people. They are perfectly free to refuse to attend his hospitals and schools, or to accept or reject his religion. He repudiates the use of force to accomplish the ends sought. It is his purpose to create a discontent for the old order of things only in so far as that old order is detrimental to the intellectual and moral advancement of the people. He presents to them that which he knows will elevate and enlarge the individual as well as make society better. It is his universal rule not to force himself or his teachings upon an unwilling people, but to leave, in every instance, the acceptance of his teachings to the good judgment of the people who hear, while they are always free to decline to listen to him at all. He never attempts to destroy, or even to condemn, anything that is good in their ancient customs or beliefs, but he simply offers to the Oriental all that he regards as best in the religion of Christ, which has created the best, and safest, and most benevolent society on earth, and has power to adapt itself to the requirements of every race and people. If we condemn the Christian foreign missionary, we must also condemn a thousandfold more the merchant missionary.

ILLUSTRATIVE QUOTATIONS

1. *Professor Gaston Bonet-Maury:* "We have a well-founded right to say that the most certain and effectual agent of civilization is the missionary."

2. *President McKinley, at the New York Ecumenical Missionary Conference, 1900:* "Who can estimate their [the missionaries'] value to the progress of the nations? Their contribution to the onward and upward march of humanity is beyond all calculation. They have inculcated industry and taught the various trades. They have promoted concord and amity, and brought nations and races closer together. They have made men better.

They have increased the regard for home; have strengthened the sacred ties of family; have made the community well ordered, and their work has been a potent influence in the development of law and the establishment of government. Wielding the sword of the Spirit, they have conquered ignorance and prejudice. They have been among the pioneers of civilization. They have illumined the darkness of idolatry and superstition with the light of intelligence and truth. They have been messengers of righteousness and love. They have braved disease, and danger, and death, and in their exile have suffered unspeakable hardships, but their noble spirits have never wavered."

3. *Hon. T. R. Jernegan, Consul-General of United States at Shanghai:* " If considered from a commercial point of view, missionary work has accomplished advantages to trade which the present awakening of China will soon evidence to be of great practical value. China can no longer sleep. The agencies of a civilization whose progress knows no receding ebb, are busily at work within the empire. Civil engineers are now mapping the vast territory of China, and tracing lines for contemplated railroads closely following his [the missionary's] tracks across plains and mountains, and by these tracks the business man pilots his ventures to the far interior marts. In the absence of the information furnished by the missionary, many of the trade marts of China would be still unfamiliar to the merchant, and demands for his merchandise confined to narrower limits. It should be remembered that the ensign of commerce follows close in the wake of the banner of the Cross, and he who would strike down the hand that carries the latter, injures the interests of the former."

4. *Chief Justice Sir Charles St. Julian of Fiji:* "If the work done by the Wesleyan Missionary Society had only been to cause the natives to cast off bad practices and customs, it would have been a very gratifying result, but the mission has built up a kingdom."

5. *From the London "Times":* "We owe it to our missionaries that the whole region [South Africa] has been opened up. Apart from their special services as preachers, they have done important work as pioneers of civilization, as geographers, as contributors to philological research. The progress of South Africa has been mainly due to men of Moffatt's stamp."

6. *From the "Review of Reviews":* "It is our brave contingent of missionary teachers, and not the present greedy squad of German and Spanish traders and officials, who have annexed the islands of the Pacific to civilization. Many of them have been completely transformed by the missionaries, whose labors long have given them commercial importance."

7. *General James H. Wilson, U. S. A., of the American forces in Peking:* "Our missionaries, after the early Jesuits, were almost the first in that wide field [China]. They were generally men of great piety and learning, like Morrison, Brown, Martin, and Williams, and did all in their power as genuine men of God to show the heathen that the stranger was not necessarily a public enemy, but might be an evangel of a higher and better civilization. These men and their co-laborers have established hospitals, schools, and colleges in various cities and provinces of the empire, which are everywhere

20

recognized by intelligent Chinese as centers of unmitigated blessing to the people. Millions of dollars have been spent in this beneficent work, and the result is slowly but surely spreading the conviction that foreign arts and sciences are superior to *'fung shuy'* and native superstition."

8. *Mr. Charles Darwin, naturalist:* "The success of the mission in Terra Del Fuego is most wonderful, and charms me, as I always prophesied utter failure. I could not have believed that all the missionaries in the world could have made the Fuegians honest. The mission is a grand success."

9. *Mr. R. Fulton Cutting of New York:* "The missionary is the advance agent of business organization and of a higher civilization. He is the apostle of law and order. Although he does not go to non-Christian lands for the purpose, it is inevitable that he should lay foundations broad and deep for their commercial future. Christianity is the great liberator from the tyranny of force."

10. *Li Hung Chang, China's greatest statesman:* "The missionaries have not sought for pecuniary gain at the hands of our people. They have not been secret emissaries of diplomatic schemes. Their labors have no political significance, and last, but not least, if I might be permitted to add, they have not interfered with or usurped the rights of territorial authorities. A man is composed of soul, intellect, and body. I highly appreciate that your eminent Boards [Foreign Missionary Boards of the United States] in your arduous and most

esteemed work in China, have neglected none of the three."

11. *Professor Edward C. Moore, Ph. D., D. D., Harvard University:* " Some nations, as some individuals, are religiously and morally better off than others in order that they may help others. . . . If we undermine their old religions and give them nothing but the secular aspects of our civilization, have we conferred such a great benefit? Are our own luxurious classes the best? . . . Missions have opened up all these countries to commerce and manufactures, and civilization is going to them. Secularization and materialization are going to take the place of their paganism. What can we do for these nations? Hold up the standard of moral earnestness and spiritual vitality. In the Indian Empire and Japan, civilization is an unmixed curse unless the moral influence of Christianity goes with it."

12. *Hon. John Barrett, journalist and United States Minister and Consul-General to Siam,* etc.: " Going out to Asia seven years ago as United States Minister to Siam, I was in a degree prejudiced against missionaries. Returning to America six years later, I was convinced of the practical value and importance of their work. Four years' official residence in Siam, a year or more in China and Japan, and another in the Philippines, aroused me to an appreciation of America's mighty responsibilities and opportunities, missionary and commercial, in the Far East. Summarizing in briefest terms possible some points in favor of missionary work from a layman's point of view, we enumerate the following:

" (1.) In my experience as a United States Minister, 150 missionaries, scattered over a land as large as the

German Empire, gave me less trouble in five years than 15 business men or merchants gave me in five months.

" (2.) Everywhere they go, in Siam or Burmah, in China or Japan, they tend to raise the moral tone of the community where they settle.

" (3.) They are the pioneers in education, starting the first practical schools and higher institutions of learning, teaching along lines that develop the spirit of true citizenship as well as of Christianity.

" (4.) They develop the idea of patriotism, of individual responsibility in the welfare of the State.

" (5.) They carry on an extensive medical and surgical work, build hospitals, and encourage sanitary measures, and have been the chief agency throughout Asia to check the spread of diseases like smallpox, cholera, and the plague.

" (6.) They do a great work of charity and teach the idea of self-help among the masses otherwise doomed to starvation and cruel slavery.

" (7) They are helpful in preparing the way for legitimate commercial expansion, and almost invariably precede the merchant in penetrating the interior.

" (8.) They have done more than either commerce or diplomacy to develop respect for American character and manhood among the countless ignorant millions of Asia.

" (9.) They are a necessity to the Asiatic statesmen and people to provide them with that instruction and information required to undertake genuine progress and development.

"Let us be fair in judging the missionaries. Let the complaining merchant, traveler, or clubman take the beam from his own eye before he demands that the mote be taken from the missionary's eye."

13. *Mr. Bosschart, Dutch Minister to Persia:* "All the rest of us are here to make money. The missionaries are here to do good. It is the noblest work in Persia."

14. *Hugh Mason, M. P.:* "I look upon the Christian missionary as the pioneer of commercial enterprise, and many a market in distant parts of the globe would have been closed for years and years to the introduction of the manufactures of Lancashire, if it had not been that devoted missionaries had first led the way in an attempt to raise the heathen in the scale, not only of Christian position, but of social position."

15. *Colonel Charles Denby, LL. D., for thirteen years United States Minister to China:* "It seems to me that no impartial observer of the work in non-Christian countries will doubt that its influence is beneficial to the Chinese as well as to the peoples of the West. When a savage or semi-civilized people become completely civilized, new wants arise which commerce supplies. . . . To the ordinary foreigner, whether a tourist or a resident, the native is a stranger, but the missionary is his constant companion and friend, and always the dispenser of charity. The missionary, too, is the forerunner of commerce. Inspired by holy zeal, he goes into the interior where the white man's foot has never trod. He builds a little chapel, a dispensary, a schoolhouse, a workshop. He effects a lodgment in the heart of the country. The drummer follows behind, and foreign commerce begins. From the missionary dwelling there radiates the light of modern civilization.

"I grant that the Imperial Maritime Customs, the diplomatic and consular bodies, the merchants, and the mariners, have done a great deal—the greater part—in the opening up of China, but the unostentatious, laborious missionary has done his full share. In general, the merchant cares little about diffusing mental or moral improvement, and still less about religion. . . . In the great question of commercial expansion the labors of the missionaries in all parts of the world have been appreciated by intelligent rulers, and they have consequently been fostered and protected."

16. *The Hon. Chester Holcombe, diplomat and author:* " It might further be added that unselfish men and devoted women, enthusiastic in what appears, to them at least, to be a great cause, who are ready to expatriate themselves and to abandon all their ambitions and their lives to its promotion in foreign lands, have as good a right to carry out their self-sacrificing wishes, to enter China and do their chosen work there by all proper methods, as have their fellow citizens who seek the same Empire in order to win a fortune by dealing in cotton goods, kerosene, silk, tea, or possibly in opium. They have precisely the same right, no greater and no less, to the protection and sympathetic assistance of their own government as any other class of citizens. To more than this, American missionaries have never made claim.

" Every missionary is, whether willingly or unwillingly, an agent for the display and recommendation of American fabrics and wares of every conceivable sort. Each missionary home, whether established in great Chinese cities or rural hamlets, serves as an object lesson, an exposition of the practical comfort, convenience, and value of the thousand and one items in the long catalogue of articles which complete the equipment of an American home. Idle curiosity upon the part of the natives grows into personal interest, which in turn develops the desire to possess. Did space permit, an overwhelming array of facts and figures could be set forth to prove the inestimable, though unrecognized, value of the missionary as an agent for the development of American commerce in every part of the globe. The manufacturing and commercial interests in the United States, even though indifferent or actively hostile to the direct purpose of the missionary enterprise, could well afford to bear the entire cost of all American missionary effort in China for the sake of the large increase in trade which results from such effort."

17. *Thomas H. Norton, Ph. D., United States Consul at Harpoot and Smyrna, Turkey:* "At present we see the map of Asiatic Turkey dotted with the stations and sub-stations, the schools, hospitals and orphanages of the American Mission. It is difficult to find a town where a school under American auspices has not been started, or to enter a village without encountering some one educated in an American school. Thousands of the orphans resulting from the massacres of 1895 and 1896 have been trained in American orphanages. The small band of American mission physicians have done untold good in the country, and the work of the finely equipped American Medical College at Beirut, in training up a large corps of skilled native physicians, is of incalculable value.

"It is not necessary to pronounce the eulogy of this widespread activity. Bryce and other British statesmen have bestowed upon it their meed of praise, and unhesitatingly ranked it as the most important factor in the evolution of a new Turkey. They have, however, failed to consider an equally important result attained, unintentionally, but no less securely, as the outcome of these many years of altruistic effort. This is the very pronounced receptive attitude of the vast masses of the population of Turkey, in regard to American ideas, methods and wares.

"Briefly stated, there is a widespread confidence in American integrity and straightforwardness, in American ways of doing business, in American wares and commercial enterprise, in American practicability and conveniences for every day life. It has been gained by the contact for two or three generations with exceptionally fine types of our countrymen, exemplifying in their own lives, in their homes, in their standards, the qualities which best win confidence in this land. It must not be forgotten that the object lesson of a single American family, with its domestic life, its practical, up-to-date conveniences for home comfort, far outweighs in advertising value the influence coming from a hundred cloistered monks or nuns.

"The general confidence slowly gained amongst certain classes, by years of patient educational or missionary effort, has been enormously supplemented of late by the extensive work of American physicians, who have entered closely into contact with other classes of the population, especially Moslems."

II

THE MISSIONARY AND NATIVE RELIGIONS

NOT long since, a prominent pastor of one of the leading churches in New England said, "If I were a foreign missionary, I would not attack the religion of the people to whom I was sent, but I would endeavor to make them feel that I was their best friend, and the religion of Jesus Christ so supremely beautiful that they would seek to know more of it." These words, together with the context, gave the impression that the speaker believed that missionaries attack the religions of the people to whom they are sent, and by their acts and teaching make Christianity repulsive. These words sounded more strange to the foreign missionaries than to any other class, for the idea combated is one to which they, for the most part, are strangers.

There is no doubt that the impression is widespread, that the first and chief duty and occupation of foreign missionaries is to attack local religions, and almost compel the people to accept Christianity. There has been enough foundation for this assumption to give those who are inclined to believe it confidence in their position. In the earlier days of missions, when there was little knowledge of the non-Christian religions, there was a wide-spread belief that everything in regard to them was wholly evil. Among the missionaries there were some who were more zealous than wise, and more religious than Christian, and consequently idols were sometimes removed from their places, and other acts committed which the people themselves regarded as indignities to their gods. In modern times, probably in every mission field, one can learn, by diligent inquiry, of cases where young missionaries, of great zeal and little education, have at some time in the past done something of the kind. But these cases are so uncommon as to excite comment at once, and call forth the universal disapproval of all wise, experienced, and sober missionaries.

It is not so uncommon for a new native convert to Christianity to express outwardly the first impulses of his new-found faith by heaping some indignity upon his old religion, either by act or word. Missionaries often find it difficult to curb the enthusiasm of the new converts. And yet these cases, all put together, are so limited in number that they play no real part in the propagation of the Gospel in any country. There are few old missionaries who cannot give some specific case or cases of this kind, but they are cherished as abnormal and rare instances which illustrate the mistakes of the perpetrators.

A missionary in the interior of Turkey related to the writer an instance of stoning through which he and a native preacher passed. It was caused by the attacks made by the native preacher, in a public address, upon the religion of his hearers. The missionary said, " There is no doubt that he was a good man and meant well, but his methods were so unreasonable and unchristian that we had to dismiss him from the service. He seemed to think it was a part of his message to criticise the beliefs and religious acts of his hearers." There is probably no mission board of strength and standing that would retain in its service a missionary or a native worker, who conceived it to be his duty to attack any religion or any belief. Missionaries are sent out not to destroy but to fulfill.

One needs but to consider the matter soberly and carefully to understand the absurdity of the assumption that the missionaries are primarily iconoclasts, and teachers of Christianity afterwards. Whatever motive may lead a missionary into a foreign country, and whatever expectations he may cherish as to the results of his labors there, his first aim must be to secure for himself the confidence of all classes. Without such confidence, he can have little personal influence, and can secure no real following. Confidence can be gained only by making the people understand and know that he is there for no other purpose than to do them good. The good may assume a thousand forms, but they must see it and understand it in some of its forms.

The first step to this confidence is the manifestation of the fact that he is their true friend. This means that he is a friend to each individual in matters personal, intellectual, social, and religious. It requires time, and patience, and persistent effort to win this position among an Oriental people who are naturally suspicious of the motives of one who professes an altruistic purpose in his labors among them. In some countries a generation of effort passed before there were marked indications of success.

Oriental people are, in many respects, the most sensitive to criticism along the lines of their ancient customs and religion. Any act of the missionary that would admit of interpretation in terms of religious hostility would set him apart as an enemy. Under these circumstances, the religious life of all with whom he came into contact would be concealed from him, and his religious influence would be practically destroyed. It requires no argument or demonstration to show that it would be futile, and even destructive of missionary effort, to use any form of attack against the religions or the religious life of the people. Observation upon the ground in different countries makes this even more apparent.

Take for instance the missionary work in Turkey that has been going on since 1820. The two classes of people reached there are the members of the Oriental churches and the Mohammedans. For 26 years the missionary worked within the old churches, refusing to be drawn into discussions that might be interpreted as criticisms of the churches or their ecclesiastics, and insisting that those who, by reading the Bible in the vernacular, were convinced that the old churches must be reformed, should not withdraw from the church. Only after the Gregorians had expelled from their churches the readers of the New Testament in the vernacular, were the Armenians organized by the missionaries into a separate church. The organization of a Protestant church was an act of defense for those who had been cast out, and was not then a sign of opposition to the old church, nor has it been since. The Protestants in Turkey did not and do not to-day attack in any way the old churches. They are endeavoring to aid those churches to live nearer their own ideals.

In Turkey the government is Mohammedan. Had the missionaries at any time, in any way, attacked Mohammedanism, they would not have been permitted to continue in the empire. Such an attack alone would have been sufficient cause for their expulsion. The Christian missionary and the Mohammedan talk together by the hour upon matters of religion and remain upon common ground. The Moslem and the Christian agree as to the Old Testament, the Law and the Prophets, and the Psalms, and also in regard to the life, character, and teachings of Jesus Christ, and the life and teachings of the Apostles. Upon this common ground they draw nearer and nearer together, and reach at last a point where they can consider dispassionately the questions about which they may differ.

A missionary in Japan was attempting to address a theater audience that was boisterously hostile. He secured his hearing only by quoting, with a mighty voice, extracts from the Confucian classics. When a hearing was secured, he announced for his theme one of the choice sayings of the Chinese sage, and then he proceeded to prove to that audience, who were ethically Confucianists, that their lives did not tally with their beliefs. He made quotation after quotation from their own ethical standards, and showed how far behind they had fallen, and how desperately in need were they of reform. Within half an hour he had his audience entirely with him, for they all saw that, according to their own best standards, they were all miserable sinners. At this point the preacher declared that Jesus Christ had expressed the same truth in somewhat different language. He then took the words of Christ and showed them how He and His disciples wrought out the same principle and gave it to the world. To every man of that audience light had come, and his own ethical teachings had been exalted and perfected in their fuller development by Christ Himself.

In India a great crowd of many religions and castes were assembled in the open air for a Christian address. The preacher knew that they were in no mood to tolerate a text from the Bible. He began by quoting from one of their well-known sacred books a common saying, declaring the necessity of a priest or intermediary for the salvation of every soul. This text was dwelt upon and illustrated from the customs of Hinduism, showing how deeply this truth is imbedded in their practices and lives. He then said, " We Christians have the same truth, in which we believe, but we call the name of our High Priest, Jesus Christ." Carefully and completely he led his hearers from the Hindu priest to the Christian's Savior, and the interest manifested in the faces of all was intense. Then he said, " We have some little books here that tell in your own language about the life and teachings of our Priest, and these can be had for two cents. All who desire can purchase." A large number bought copies of the Gospels.

These incidents are merely illustrative of the common, everyday methods of the missionaries in every land. They everywhere assume that the people for whom they are at work already have a religion. They endeavor to become as familiar as possible with the religious thinking of the races around them, and to understand their beliefs, superstitions, and acts of worship. When rightly understood and interpreted, every religion is a preparation, in greater or less degree, for the preaching of Christianity.

When the writer was in India, a Hindu high priest was showing him through one of their important temples. A Protestant missionary was in the company. The priest spoke English easily and was voluble in his talk. Early in his conversation, he was describing one of the gods before whom we stood, when the missionary most adroitly and kindly asked him if he was not confusing the name of the god he was describing with one standing several feet away. He hesitated a moment, said the missionary was right, and then went on correctly. Frequently after that, he consulted the missionary openly in regard to an idol, or a legend, or some principle of Hinduism. Quietly he said to the writer during the hour in the temple, " These missionaries study our religion more thoroughly than the most of us do, and so come to know it much more accurately."

It is of supreme value for a people to be devoutly

religious, even if that devotion is wholly misdirected. Races in whom the spirit of worship has been strongly developed and maintained are more devout when they come to worship the true God. In India one sees countless cases of worshipers who appear to devote their whole being to the act of worship, in which they suffer hardship, peril, and even death. Palsied be the tongue that would destroy this sense of devotion and faculty for worship. The Christian missionary's task is but gently to lead such out under clear skies and to teach the worshiper to look beyond his images up into the face of his God and living Father. The image will soon lose its value to one who has learned to commune directly with his God.

The Hindu is burdened with an overwhelming sense of evil. He feels the heavy hand of his gods upon him, and in a thousand ways he turns that he may escape. Oppressive vows are taken, pilgrimages entered upon, sacrifices offered, temples visited, holy places drawn upon, but without avail. The Christian missionary sits down with the despairing soul and tenderly but gradually leads him on beyond the temples and shrines, and points him to the Lamb of God that taketh away the sins of the world. He has to meet frequently the same question that confronted Paul upon Mars Hill, when he declared to the Athenians the God whom they worshiped in ignorance.

It is undoubtedly true that there is no religion in mission lands which does not provide a basis upon which to begin to teach Christianity. It is not the purpose or desire of the missionaries to destroy the religion of the one whom he would teach, but to enrich, enlarge, and fulfil it, as Christ Himself did the religion of the Jews. This does not mean, and can never mean, that the missionary compromises with his hearers and gives them a diluted form of Christianity. It does mean that he takes full cognizance of all that is good and true in the religion of the people to whom he goes, and endeavors, from that starting point, to lead them on to a full personal knowledge of the true God, and to Jesus Christ as Redeemer and Lord.

It often requires great care and thoughtfulness upon the part of the missionary not to be led by the enlightened people themselves to take a position that would allow of a hostile interpretation. A sincere inquirer, a member of an Oriental church, said to a missionary, "You do not pray to pictures and our priests do; why do you not do it?" The missionary replied, "I do not pray to pictures because I can find no command in the Bible to do so, or anything that leads me to believe that such a practice will help me." The next question followed with exactness, "Why, then, do our priests teach us to pray to pictures?" The missionary's reply was, "I do not know; you must ask the priests, not me. They probably have a reason which they can explain to you."

Another man in Catholic lands said to a missionary, "You have never failed to teach us the necessity of our living pure lives, if we would be genuinely Christian, and you find reasons for your teachings in the Bible. If what you say is true, why do so many of our celibate priests and higher clergy have such large families?" The missionary refused to be drawn into a discussion of the lives and characters of the priests and clergy. He replied that it is no part of his work or office to criticise the lives of leaders in the Church.

Such questions constantly arise, and are as persistently put aside in order that the main issue be not clouded. The missionary's gospel is a positive one, and would only be weakened were the preacher to turn aside to vent his feelings and prejudices, or to attack a person of whose life he does not approve. Thus missionaries, by keeping themselves from controversy, deepen and strengthen the influence and power of their message upon all classes.

In spite of this position and practice, which fairly illustrate the work of the great body of missionaries representing the old and leading mission boards, it is inevitable that among certain classes severe opposition to the missionary should develop. The priest, to whom the people bring their troublesome questions regarding images, pictures, penance, and purity of life, does not feel kindly toward the man who teaches truths in the light of which his life as a priest seems even to himself mean and unworthy. When Christian churches have multiplied, and, in consequence thereof, the revenues of the temples begin to fall off, the temple keepers cannot feel kindly towards the men whose preaching and lives have contributed to that result. When the general standard of education, through mission and government schools, has so risen that the people are no longer satisfied as they formerly were with their ignorant religious leaders, and are beginning to express that dissatisfaction in many ways, it is not to be expected that those leaders will have any sympathy with a religion that demands and provides for the intellectual elevation of the masses. It is evident that natural opposition to the fundamental principles of Christianity is inevitable. Whenever and wherever light and darkness come together, a conflict invariably ensues. Righteousness, purity, and right-living necessarily must cause injustice and vulgarity to rage, and whoever stands for these principles of the Christian life must bring down upon himself hatred and abuse. This is true in every land and among all peoples: it is pre-eminently true in non-Christian countries.

If the facts were fully understood, it would appear that most of the opposition to missionaries in any country arises from officials of existing religious orders, or from those to whom the fundamental principles of Christian living are a constant reproach. In numbers, those who openly oppose the Christian missionary are but a handful compared with the multitude who welcome and trust him.

The missionary, therefore, in his work and teaching does not attempt to overthrow or suppress anything that is good and true in the lives, and beliefs, and practices of the people. By his teaching, through his life as well as his words, he endeavors to make evil appear so undesirable, and good so exalting and beautiful, that all shall hate evil and choose the good. He teaches the people the goodness and the love of God in all their length and breadth and power, until their own circumscribed religion, in comparison, appears like a taper in the glare of the noonday sun. There is no need, then, to explain how feeble is the light of the taper. In this way every religion finds its fulfilment in absorption into that which is supreme. All that is good in the old religion remains, all else disappears. The missionary does not forget that Jesus Christ came not to destroy, but to fulfil.

ILLUSTRATIVE QUOTATIONS

1. *D. L. Leonard, D. D., Associate Editor of the " Missionary Review of the World ":* " No conception of history can be nobler or more inspiring than this, that it is the portrayal of the marvelous process of lifting mankind from the groveling, the earthly, and the bestial, up to the celestial and divine; from savagery to civilization, from despotism and slavery to republican freedom, from the puerilities and abominations of paganism to the spiritual worship of a heavenly Father."

2. *Henry W. Longfellow:*
   " To rescue souls forlorn and lost,
      The troubled, tempted, tempest-tost,
   To heal, to comfort, and to teach;
      The fiery tongues of Pentecost
   His symbols were, that they should preach
      In every form of human speech,
      From continent to continent."

3. *Deputation of the A. B. C. F. M. to India and Ceylon:* " The esteem in which our missonaries are held by the masses of the people, and by many leading Hindus

and Mohammedans and others, was apparent. We were handed many written addresses, in which the deepest respect for the personal character and work of the missionaries was strongly expressed. The same appeared in private conversation and in the relations which existed between these people and the missionary body. We did not expect to find the missionary influence so widely extended outside of the Christian circles, or themselves held in such high esteem by leading natives of all classes. The same can be said of the attitude of the English officials whom we met."

4. *Extract from an address read to the American Board Deputation in June, 1901, from "The Sivite Community" of Tillipally in Jaffna, Ceylon:* "During the eight decades since you began work here, excellent results have been produced upon the people at large. We beg to render the Board, through you, our heartfelt thanks for the blessings of education, culture, and civilization that have inevitably attended the preaching of the Gospel here. The noble ideals of duty and purity of life which have been set before the people of this country by the exemplary lives led by your missionaries have elevated our character and infused a spirit of charity and gentleness into many a Sivite home, and the many moral precepts from the Scriptures, taught us in our Bible classes, have been so well impressed upon us that they have been the underlying principles of guidance to us in matters of our daily life."

5. *The Asiatic Quarterly Review,* speaking of missionaries with whom it was not much in sympathy, calls them "An unrivalled disintegrating force. True alchemists, possessors of the philosopher's stone. Is this *magnum*

opus, on which the teaching of several hundred sects converge, a small matter? Is it naught to take the base metal, the outward civilization, the pomp and riches from the heathen and to convert this dross for his benefit into blessings everlasting?"

6. *Indian Messenger (Brahmo Somaj)*: "Famine work must not close without a word of recognition of the valuable services rendered by Christian missionaries toward mitigating its horrors. Honor to these ambassadors of Christ! They have proved themselves to be worthy followers of Him whose heart bled for the sorrows of men. For the last six months every mission station in the Central Provinces, in Gujarat, and in many parts of the Western Presidency, was converted into a relief camp. The missionary workers did not know rest, but were out day and night relieving distress and saving lives. The strain was so severe that one of these workers writes: 'Every mission in these parts has lost at least one European worker by death, and ours one each month for the last four months.' Not only did these workers offer themselves as a sacrifice, but money also flowed freely for the relief of distress from Christian centers in this country and abroad. Verily, Christian philanthropy comes to us with healing balm for the many afflictions. This humanity of Jesus' followers, and not their dogmas, will surely establish the throne of their Master on the love and reverence of civilized humanity. Let all classes of Indian society record their admiration to these worthy servants of Christ in unstinted measure."

7. *William Hayes Ward, LL. D., Editor of the New York "Independent"*: I believe the work of the foreign

missionary to be the best and wisest done for the Kingdom of God and the uplifting of the human race. They are everywhere the friends of the people with whom they labor; believers in their capacity for development; their defenders against race prejudice, and often Anglo-Saxon arrogance and contempt; their teachers who show them to what they can attain, the one uplifting influence among them in China, in Turkey, in Africa. It is foreign missions more than anything else, I fully believe, that civilizes the world while it Christianizes."

8. *Orthodox Hindu Paper, published in Bombay, India:* "Whether the Hindu religion is being injured by the missionaries or not; or whether by their work amongst orphans the Christian religion is being advanced or not, we cannot possibly withhold our praise of the missionaries. In the famine of 1900 the missionaries, and especially the Americans, saved the lives of thousands of India's inhabitants. By their money, zeal, and toil vast numbers of orphans are saved forever from the claws of famine and poverty and are receiving instruction in handicrafts."

9. *Correspondent to the Boston "Herald," in Mexico:* "To go back to the missionaries. They are useful in their educational work, they do good when they help open the eyes of poor, degraded, and neglected beings to spiritual things, and in their example of correct living they counteract, in remote districts, the bad example of slothful priests who have forgotten, if ever they comprehended, their divine mission. Where the dominant church is lax the Protestant missionaries are an embodied rebuke. They bring in the competition of religions, and set the native clergy to thinking that they must get nearer the poor than is possible in church ceremonies."

10. *Indian Social Reformer:* "If you wish to find examples of the noblest benevolence, you must go to Christianity and not to Hinduism,—the highest types of Christian character yet evolved by our race were found among some of the Christian missionaries of India."

11. *Extract from an address read to the American Board Deputation at Madura, India, by Judge Varado Rao Avergal, B. A., B. L., Assistant Sessions Judge of Madura:* "Whenever I am transferred on official duty to a new district, it is with a feeling of relief that I hear that the missionary is at work in that special field of labor. We Hindus are not so blind or bigoted as not to recognize the manifold good results flowing from the adoption of the Christian faith by some of the communities which form the population of Southern India."

12. *Extract from an address read to the American Board Deputation in Madura, India, by W. W. Subramania Iyer, Editor:* "The names of your missionaries became household words in this district by the love and sympathy they almost invariably bring to bear upon every department of their work. . . . A silent and wonderful revolution is taking place in Indian minds, and many in India are imbued with Christian spirit, and breathing Christian thoughts, and adopting Christian modes of charity, which would have been a phenomenon a few years ago."

13. *From an address read to the American Board Deputation by Mr. Tirumalia Pillai, Special Deputy Collector, India:* "The last and most important of the work done by the missionaries is the elevation of the

moral tone and sense of duty, imbibed in the midst of my countrymen by free intercourse and friendship with them. The missionaries are easily accessible to all, and are freely consulted in all matters, even on domestic affairs, by Hindus. Such contact benefits both parties, and especially the latter. The general impression was, and is, that the fact of a man being a Christian was a guarantee to his truth-speaking and good conduct. The teaching in the schools, public preaching and private contact with our revered missionaries, go a great way toward molding the character of my countrymen. In brief, gentlemen, the work done by your mission is of incalculable benefit to India, and it cannot be sufficiently thankful to your kind-hearted countrymen. What we want and pray for is more extended work."

14. *A non-Christian writer in the Indian "Spectator":* "It is not true that Christianity has been successful only among the very lowest classes of Indian society. A careful survey of the Indian Christian community will show how much of truth there is in the above statement. According to Professor Christlieb's estimate, in India, out of every six converts one comes of a higher caste or class; and when we consider the highly organized religious creeds, the deeply rooted social prejudices and customs, and that subtlest and that most inflexible of foes, caste, which Christian missionaries have to cope with when dealing with high-caste Hindus, the success that has already attended their efforts is itself a triumph of Christianity. We, of course, admit that those classes of the Indian population least influenced by the subtle, stereotyping influence of Hindu culture and the Hindu religion have become most accessible to Christianity. But what is the result? It is those very classes, despised,

trampled down, and looked upon as utterly incapable of improvement of any kind, that now, with the enlightening influence of Christianity, compete successfully with the highest castes and classes of Indian society in every direction—morally, socially, and intellectually. In our opinion, even if there had not been a single convert from the higher classes of Hindu society, the transformation which Christianity has wrought among the lower classes that it has won over to its fold, is a clear evidence of its unique triumph in this country."

15. *A non-Christian Japanese:* "The missionaries have lived good, honest lives, and been careful not to give occasion for scandal; the native Christians, as a rule, have in their lives been consistent with their profession. It was a very great and noteworthy thing that there should be these men and women from the Far West to represent to us the ethical and spiritual side of their civilization. By their very presence they remind us of the importance of morality and religion in the life of the nation."

16. *An Educated Hindu:* "I have given the subject of social reform my best thought and attention these twelve years. My conviction is that the liberal education of women and the consequent happiness of the home is possible only in the Christian community. It is Christianity that permits the postponement of the marriage of girls. It is Christianity that allows widows to remarry. It is Christianity that gives fallen women a chance of reclaiming themselves from evil ways. It is Christianity that allows foreign travel. It is Christianity that teaches the dignity of labor. It is Christianity that allows all facilities for being rich, wise, and philan-

thropic. It is Christianity that gives free scope for women to receive complete education. It is Christianity that gives salvation without the laborious and multifarious ceremonies. If ever the Hindus are to rise in the scale of nations, it must be by Christianity, and Christianity only. Some of my Hindu brothers may say that agnosticism or atheism may produce these results; but I do not believe in that. Man cannot do without religion."

17. *Pweushotam Rao Telang, a Brahman:* " In justice to the missionary, I must say that he has done much to lift the Pariah, socially and mentally, by opening schools and educating those who become converts. The structure of Hindu society and religion—built on caste—is such that here is no such help for the Pariah as the Christian missionary has brought to him."

III

THE MISSIONARY AND THE TOURIST

THE term "tourist" is here used of one who makes a hasty trip through foreign lands, covering much territory, seeing many things, but investigating little or nothing. Some of the best people in the world travel in this way. Many of them are devout Christians, and not unbelievers in missions. The pressure under which these people travel, and the scant time allowed at the great capitals where so many objects of Oriental interest are found, preclude the possibility of much investigation of missionary operations in these places. There is no time for it without sacrificing the very object of the trip, or without a complete change of the program such as is practically impossible in most cases. Often the traveler sets out with the expectation of personally inspecting some mission stations; but weariness begotten of perpetual sight-seeing, and the unexpected number of objects of general interest to be seen, and Oriental shops to be searched through, shut out the missionary and his work from a ghost of a chance of a hearing, and may entirely exclude him from the mind. There are some who feel that, after the interest and excitement of the general sight-seeing, to turn aside and see mission work would be terribly tame, if not an actual bore. They have little or no real conception of what that work is, and do not feel ready to give an opportunity to the missionary to exhibit it. Many think it consists largely of prayer meetings, or some form of religious services, in which the travelers would be expected to take a part, from which they shrink, and which they avoid by absenting themselves entirely. If these people could only see the schools of all grades, the hospitals and dispensaries, the industrial schools and kindergartens, the printing establishments, colleges and theological seminaries, they would know that in many respects these institutions themselves are more of a marvel than many of the things people go half around the world to see.

Not a few go into Oriental cities where they know mission work is carried on by their own Board, fully intending to call upon a missionary, to whom it is possible they have a letter of introduction, or it may be whom they once knew. At the hotel they inquire about the missionaries, and are informed with a kind of half sneer, " Yes, there are some missionaries in the city, but nobody thinks much of them. They do not go in good society and are not accomplishing much of anything." The chances are that this will be followed by some stock stories about missionaries which float about all Oriental ports, many of them earmarked with age, until the would-be visitor decides not to call, and comes away keenly disappointed that missionaries are really such low-down people, and the work they are attempting such an utter failure. Some of the most damaging reports about missionary work brought back to this country by travelers come from those who never saw a missionary abroad, or set eyes upon missionary operations of any kind.

A Christian gentleman, a business man, told the writer that, with a party of tourists, he once visited Constantinople, where they were scheduled for ten days. One of his beloved college classmates was at that time a missionary in Turkey and located at that port. He did not let the missionary know he was coming, but planned to surprise him by taking him unawares. Nine days were spent in sight-seeing, during which time he made no little inquiry regarding missionary work. The guide told him the missionaries were a lot of fanatics, who had gained no foothold in the empire, but who, by deceiving the constituency at home through false reports, were kept on there, and thus they secured their living, which they would not be able to do at home.

The gentleman was much disturbed, because he felt sure his missionary friend would be greatly embarrassed to have him call and discover, by personal observation, the hollow failure of his work. He would not have called at all but for fear it would later be known he had visited the Porte. On the forenoon of the last day of the visit, he called at the Bible House and found his old classmate. He was impressed with the happy expression he wore, and with the signs of activity about the Bible House. After the first greetings the missionary asked, " Have you just arrived in the city?"

" No," was the reply, " we came nine days ago, and are just leaving."

It was hard to explain why the call upon his old chum was so long delayed, but as this was not the first experience of the missionary in this line, he changed the subject, and asked,

" What have you seen of the missionary work? "

" I have seen nothing," was the reply. " I fear I shall have to go home without seeing it at all."

" What have you heard about missionary work? " asked the missionary. " What kind of an impression are you taking away of missionary operations in this city? "

The friend was compelled to reply, " I have the impression that there is no real work here that is worth seeing and which can be shown, and I do not wish to embarrass you by making you feel that you must try to show me something."

The missionary, a man of decision, replied, " You cannot leave this city with that impression. It is absolutely false, and your own sense of justice must compel you to permit me to prove to you that your impression is entirely wrong. You shall not go this afternoon."

Arrangements were made, and while the party went on, the two friends began their tour of the city, searching for the fruits of missions and their institutions. The gentleman told the writer that in the four days he stayed over, he not only saw more of real value and interest in that old city than he had seen during the previous nine days, but he saw more genuine mission work than he supposed was carried on in the entire Turkish Empire. He became enthusiastic for missions, and spoke in their favor wherever he had opportunity. He also said that, had he come away as he had planned to do, he would never have had any further interest in missions, but would have cherished always the idea that they are practically a failure. His testimony would have gone far, for, " had he not spent ten days in Constantinople, and did he not obtain his information first-hand ? "

Not a little of the testimony of travelers in regard to the extent and value of mission work is the same that this gentleman's would have been had he left the city in ignorance, and at the same time prejudiced. The cases are far too few where the missionary has any chance whatever to eradicate the false impression by an exhibition of the facts.

A few years ago, in the city of Bombay, early one morning a missionary residing there was waited upon by a gentleman and lady from Boston. When he came to the door of the mission bungalow, in response to the summons, he found, sitting in a carriage in front of the door, a well-dressed man and woman whom he greeted with an inquiring " Good-morning ? " The lady pleasantly responded, but the gentleman, whom we will call Mr. W., gruffly asked, " Are you a missionary ? "

The missionary replied, " I am," and invited them into the house.

Mr. W. paid no attention to the invitation, but said, " You are the man we are looking for," and then con-

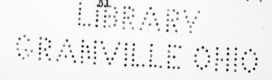

tinued, "We are upon a tour around the world. I take no stock in missions or in missionaries, but my wife does. I wanted her to come with me, but she persistently refused unless I would promise to give one day to an investigation of missions. She would not yield, therefore I promised. To-day is the day I have set apart for this business. If you have anything here in this city, show it up."

The missionary replied, "This is a week day, and the Christians are scattered all over this great city. It will be impossible to get them together upon so short notice."

"I do not suppose," interrupted Mr. W., "you ever get a congregation of Christians together in this city, so I am not disappointed. But have you anything at all to show us to-day?"

"Oh, yes," said the missionary, "I can show you a number of Christian schools."

"Jump right in here, and we will start at once so as to have it over with as soon as possible," commanded Mr. W., and the missionary, leaving word in the bungalow, obeyed.

They visited the smaller schools first, where little dark-eyed boys and girls were taught by Christian native teachers. The pupils went through various exercises, which the gentleman well knew were not prepared especially for his coming.

In one school of about eighty pupils, Mr. W. sat where he could look into the faces of the pupils, and, at the same time, watch the crowd of boys and girls collected in the street in front of the door, watching the strangers. He seemed to arouse from his attitude of indifference, and, after close observation, said, "Of course, these children in the school are of quite a different and higher caste from those in the street about the door?"

"No," replied the missionary, "they are all of the same caste. The difference you see is due to the influence of the Christian school, which demands cleanliness and awakens and arouses the intellects of the children."

In the industrial department of a large orphanage he again revealed interest, in spite of his studied effort not to do so.

After tiffin, they went to the mission high school, where were over three hundred dark-skinned boys and girls who were receiving Christian instruction, largely under native Christian teachers. Here English was used to a large extent, and the travelers found much more to command their admiration. After more than an hour of impromptu exercises, nearly one hundred of the pupils, all of them dark-eyed sons and daughters of India, assembled in one corner of the large schoolroom, with a native teacher presiding at a small "baby organ." There, with no score before them, and accompanied only by the little organ, they rendered the Hallelujah chorus of Handel's "Messiah," "Hallelujah, hallelujah, the Lord God omnipotent reigneth, and he shall reign forever and ever. Hallelujah."

They finished and had taken their seats before a movement was made on the part of the spectators, except that Mr. W. was seen to brush his eyes with a rapid sweep of his hand. The silence was broken by the gruff voice of the traveler to the missionary, "You ought to have a better organ for that exercise."

The missionary quietly replied, "We would like a better one, but this does very well when we become accustomed to it."

Mr. W. answered, "It is entirely inadequate, entirely inadequate. I will send you a better one when I get home." Then, remembering himself, he turned to his wife and said, "My dear, I do not believe in missions any more than I ever did, but I believe in this kind of work, and such as we have seen to-day. This is not missions; it is straight, civilizing Christian work."

The organ came, a fine one, and each year, so long as the gentleman lived, he sent that missionary a check of not less than three figures, and each time he wrote, "I do not believe in missions any more than I ever did, but I believe in you and the work you are doing there in Bombay."

One trouble is that, like this gentleman, many travelers, as well as others, have formed a preconception of what they think constitutes mission work in which they do not believe. The chances are that no missionary or secretary of a mission board would believe in their idea of the work any more than they do. It is to correct such false conceptions that visits to the field are necessary, and it is for the same purpose that the following evidence is exhibited.

It should also be stated that the most progressive and

attractive work of missions is not at the ports, but in the interior of the country. The ports are the very hardest places to work in, and show the least results for the effort put forth. This has been and is so notoriously true that some have proposed putting forth little effort to Christianize the great coast cities of the Orient, centering strength and forces upon interior stations. These cities are where the worst elements of the Occident and the Orient meet, and the evil of the one arouses and even begets a worse evil in the other. It would not do, however, to neglect these most needy centers simply because they are so needy. This would be cowardly, and could not fail to invite merited criticism and even censure. Native Christians from the interior go to the coast cities for purposes of trade and business, while in some countries the high native official classes obtain their only knowledge of missions and missionaries from what they see of them in the large towns. But if one wishes to see missions in their strength and glory, he must push past the ports into the interior of the country. If he wishes to see this work in its best and purest form, and the natives uncontaminated with the evils of the West, he must go to those points where the foreign traveler and adventurer have scarcely penetrated.

The missionaries are glad to welcome the traveler, especially the Christian traveler who is willing to see and inspect the work done. There is a certain peril in too brief an inspection, for a superficial survey may give a false impression. But even this is far better than forming an adverse judgment without any inspection whatever, and reporting that judgment at home to the injury of the work. No person, after a visit to the Orient, has a right to report that missions are a failure unless he has investigated them himself, or secured testimony from trustworthy persons who have made such investigation. Many a Christian man is ready to condemn missionaries and missions upon evidence that he, if a judge, would not consider sufficient to impose a fine of ten dollars upon a prisoner at the bar.

After nearly twenty years' close connection with missionaries and missionary work around the world, I can say that I have never seen a person who has looked into the work of missionaries and inspected that work with any degree of thoroughness, who did not testify to his belief in its wisdom, economy, efficiency, and power. I have never heard this work condemned by one who did not confess, when pressed, that he had never seen the work, nor did he have testimony to offer that would be accepted in any court as evidence sufficient to convict a horse thief. When one inveighs against foreign missions, it is always well to ask for specific cases of inefficiency and for the evidence. If these cannot be given satisfactorily, it is well to suspend judgment. We would not maintain for a moment that all of the operations of foreign missionaries are above criticism. There are inefficient missionaries, as there are inefficient ministers, lawyers, and doctors in this country. Some methods of work are open to criticism, and ought to be criticised. Mission boards do not always agree as to the best method of conducting the work in all particulars. It is inevitable that the thoughtful, careful investigator of missions will find something in every mission that he would have different. In some cases, when the work is better understood, the reasonableness of the present methods will be more fully appreciated. In other cases, the method is wrong and should be changed. This, however, is no reason for indiscriminate condemnation.

ILLUSTRATIVE QUOTATIONS

1. *Lucien C. Warner, LL. D., New York:* "Incidental to my travels in various countries I have studied the work of foreign missions in Egypt, India, Ceylon, China, and Japan. I have found that the missionaries are nearer to the natives, understand them better and can give more reliable information than any other class of foreign residents. They are, as a class, well informed, self-denying, earnest and consecrated men and women, and the work they are doing is of the highest importance in freeing the people from superstition and darkness, and giving to them the light and truth of Christianity and modern civilization. The criticism which the foreign traveler hears of missions comes very largely from those who have no personal acquaintance with the missionaries, or direct knowledge of the work they are doing. Government officials and others who study closely the conditions of the people nearly always speak well of mission work, even although not themselves professing Christians."

2. John Wanamaker, ex-Postmaster General, U. S. A.:
"While the British Government, from India's tax funds, assists India's schools, colleges, and hospitals, I found the largest proportion of humanitarian religious work going on there traceable to the Christian religion. By personal contact with the work and workers, I convinced myself that the work of the missionaries, clergymen, teachers, doctors, and Christian helpers was healthy, eminently practical, and well administered.

"In its business administration it is quite as economically done as any business firm could establish and support business extensions permanently and successfully in lands far distant from home, climate, and custom requiring different modes of living. No private business man, in my judgment, can administer from the United States properties and finances in India more effectually for less, as a rule, than the board is administering them.

"In all my life I never saw such opportunity for investment of money that anyone sets apart to give to the Christ who gave Himself for us. As I looked at the little churches, schools, and hospitals, and inquired the original cost of buildings and expense of administration, I felt a lump of regret in my heart, that I had not been wise enough to make these investments myself, and wished a hundred times I had known twenty-five years ago what I learned a half-year ago."

3. Hon. F. S. Stratton, Collector of the Port of San Francisco: "I went out opposed to the missionary movement in China, at least I had no sympathy with it. All the stock arguments against it are familiar to me. I, however, have been converted by what I have seen. America leads all others in philanthropic and religious work in the Orient, and the results, while slow, are, in my opinion, sure, and the foundation is being splendidly laid. Commercially speaking, the missionaries are the advance agents for American commercial enterprises. If business men only understood this better, they would assist rather than discourage evangelistic work in the East. The Chinese know nothing about Admiral Kempff's refusal to fire on the Taku Fort, but they know all about the eleemosynary work of the missionaries, and are grateful to America."

4. *Robert Louis Stevenson, traveler and author:* "I had conceived a great prejudice against missions in the South Seas, and I had no sooner come there than that prejudice was at first reduced, and then at last annihilated. Those who deblatterate against missions have only one thing to do, to come and see them on the spot. They will see a great deal of good done, and I believe, if they be honest persons, they will cease to complain of mission work and its effects."

5. *Captain Palmer, of the British Navy:* "Whether in the Sandwich Islands or New Zealand, amongst the Society, Fiji, or New Hebrides groups, I have ever found them [the missionaries] the same earnest, God-fearing men, striving to their utmost to win souls amongst those who, but for them, would never hear of the 'glad tidings of great joy.' They require no advocacy from me, however; I only ask those who are so fond of running down missionaries to think a little, and not talk ignorantly and wickedly about men and women whose lives adorn some of the brightest pages of British history."

6. *E. D. G. Prime (Eusebius), D. D., editor New York "Observer":* "After having embraced every opportunity

for becoming acquainted with the Christian laborers from every land, and with their work, I return with a higher estimate than I ever had before of the ability, learning and devotion of the missionaries as a class and as a whole; with an enlarged view of what has already been accomplished and with a profounder conviction that through this instrumentality, or that which shall immediately grow out of it, the kingdom of our Lord and Saviour is to be established in the whole earth more speedily than the weak faith of the church has dared even hope.

"The success of Christian missions nothing but ignorance or prejudice could call in question. What has actually been accomplished can be fully appreciated only by those who have been upon the ground, and who have witnessed the condition of pagan nations."

7. *Henry M. Field, D.D., editor New York "Evangelist"*: "My visit to India has increased my interest in missions exactly in proportion as it has increased my knowledge of them. Never have I seen more fully exemplified the inspiration of a great object and its power to raise men .above those considerations of personal care and comfort which depress less heroic natures. Who does not see that a missionary bungalow with its school, its orphanage, its church, and its daily influence of teaching and of example, is a center of civilization, when planted in the heart of an Indian village? Such a picture may be seen in hundreds of villages all over India. We must beg the pardon of our scientific friends who think the world is to be regenerated by natural philosophy, if we think a few such missionaries do more for the social and moral elevation of the people than would Professors

Tyndall and Huxley, with all the other lecturers of the Royal Institution."

8. *Rev. Francis E. Clark, D. D., Founder and President of the United Society of Christian Endeavor, in his "Journey Around the World."*

"I am glad to have my last word in this book testify to the fact that missionary work of all the various Protestant denominations in all parts of the world is, in my eyes, the most promising and hopeful feature of modern civilization. For the enlargement of commerce, for the spread of civilization, for the uplifting of humanity, for the redemption of the world, there is no such force as that which is exerted by the Anglo-Saxon missionaries of the Cross, the ministers of the Lord Jesus Christ.

"Until one travels from Canton to Kalgan and takes long journeys into the interior, one cannot realize the extent of this wonderful work, or the resourcefulness of the missionaries. Nor can one realize the hold which the missionary has upon the future of China. He has not only established churches and planted schools; he has written books and translated other books, and introduced Western arts and sciences, and pioneered the way for commerce and civilization. . . . The missionary is unsealing the Chinaman's ears, that he may hear the tramp of the advancing nations of the twentieth century."

9. *Mrs. Isabella Bird Bishop, traveler and author:* "I am a convert to missions through seeing missions and the need for them. Some years ago I took no interest whatever in the condition of the heathen; I had heard much ridicule cast upon Christian missions, and perhaps had imbibed some of the unhallowed spirit. But the missionaries, by their life and character, and by the work

they are doing, wherever I have seen them, have produced in my mind such a change and such an enthusiasm, as I might almost express it, in favor of Christian missions, that I cannot go anywhere without speaking about them and trying to influence others in their favor who may be as indifferent as I was."

10. *Henry M. Stanley, explorer.* When Mr. Stanley was asked, " Do you consider the efforts of foreign missionaries really a success? " he replied, " Yes, most emphatically. It can be shown to-day as something marvelous. The story of the Uganda missionary enterprise is an epic poem. I know of few secular enterprises, military or otherwise, deserving of greater praise."

11. *John Henry Barrows, D. D., President of Oberlin College and Haskell Lecturer to India:* " After three months in India and nearly one in Japan, wherein amplest opportunities were mine for seeing and knowing the labors of Christian propagandists in the Orient, I record my deep conviction that Christian missions in the East are more wonderful, more admirable, and better worth studying than any other feature of the life of Asia.

" I did not expect to find the work of Christian missions so varied, wise and faithful, and effective as I discovered it to be. The toil and self-sacrifice which have been put into the work of foreign missions are prodigious, and the notion that missionaries live a luxurious and self-indulgent life is the fabrication of ignorance and malice.

" I have seen enough of the practical workings of Buddhism and Hinduism and Islamism to crystallize into adamantine firmness my previous strong convictions as to their futility to give the soul abiding peace with God, to lay the sure foundations of a permanent civilization, of a permanent individual and a national morality, or to brighten earth with the sure promise of a blessed immortality; and I have seen enough of the actual workings of the Christian missions in Asia to fill me with enthusiasm and triumphant hopefulness.

"The objects most worth seeing in India, to my thinking, are neither the Himalayas, nor the Taj Mahal, the Tomb of Akbar, nor the temple of Madura, but the varied triumphs of missionary effort.

"Of course, I heard many criticisms of missionaries, but I never heard a Hindu, Brahmin, or Moslem say, what ignorant and prejudiced Europeans have sometimes said in my hearing out of India, that the missionaries were doing no good. Frequently the chairman at my lectures, or the Hindu gentleman who moved the votes of thanks, spoke with grateful appreciation of the work which missionary educators are doing. I shall never forget how the famous Hindu ascetic, the Holy Man of Benares, said to me: 'I think Jesus Christ was a very good man. He must have been something like Mr. Hewlett,' a deceased veteran of the London Missionary Society. Missionaries are often foolishly criticised by natives, but they are trusted by them, and this is the highest praise which a Hindu can pay to mortal man. I know a missionary of the American Board in southern India who was asked to take charge of the funds of one of the greatest of Hindu temples."

12. *Edward Abbott D. D.:* "There are men and women at work in obscure corners of Japan and China and India who are the peers of any that can be named. Their self-abnegation, their concentration of the highest gifts upon a remote and obscure field, their comparative

isolation, their fidelity unseen, their steadiness to the privileges in which they read their duty, furnish one of the highest types of devotedness of which history has any record.

"The more closely one looks into the mission fields, as seen in India, China, and Japan, the more carefully he studies the underground relations and influences of the truest missionary work, the more sensible does he become of the fact that the results are not to be stated in figures."

13. *Miss Clara Barton, President American Red Cross Society* (Written while engaged in Red Cross work in Turkey in 1896): "If I only had words to express the impressions these missionaries gave me of noble, devoted, self-sacrificing character, it would be a relief to me. What they endure for the loving Master's sake will never be told in words."

14. *William E. Baxter, M. P.:* "Wherever I traveled four years ago—in Egypt, Palestine, Syria, Asiatic and European Turkey,—I found that men of all nationalities and creeds, of all opinions on the Eastern question, and all questions as well, emphatically and unanimously gave evidence that the colleges, schools, churches, and other institutions conducted in the most business-like manner, with most conspicuous ability, with a remarkable freedom from all sectarian or religious narrowness, by American gentlemen, were doing more for the civilization and elevation of the ignorant masses in the East than any other agency whatever."

15. *Rev. Dillon Bronson:* "India has suffered from many invasions in the lust of blood and gold. She is now blessed with an invasion of love, and no honest

American who studies the work of our representatives in Asia at first hand can fail to thank God for it. I have seen many missionaries in many lands, but never an utterly selfish and unworthy one."

16. *Mr. H. Stonehewer Cooper:* "I cannot agree with perhaps the majority of the missionaries in the South Seas; but despite all differences of creed, I raise my hat in respectful homage, when I think what these men have done. . . . There can be no doubt of the enormous benefits which have followed the labors of Christian missionaries in the Pacific."

17. *Professor W. M. Ramsey, archaeologist:* "Beginning with a prejudice against the work of the missionaries, I was driven by the force of facts and experience to the opinion that the mission has been the strongest, as well as most beneficent, influence, in causing the movement toward civilization."

18. *Phillips Brooks, Bishop of Massachusetts:* "Tell your friends who do not believe in foreign missions (and I am sure there are a good many such) that they do not know what they are talking about, and that three weeks' sight of mission work in India would convert them wholly."

19. *Jesse Seligman, Jewish banker and traveler:* "I am glad to inform you that the American missionaries all along the Nile are doing splendid work. You can scarcely enter a single town or village without finding one of these nicely constructed schoolhouses where these Arabs are taught, and it would astonish you to hear with

what pride they say they were taught at the American Mission School."

20. *Dr. Schweinfurth, scentist and explorer:* "The American Mission in Egypt has done an enormous amount of good."

21. *The Hon. Charles Denby, LL. D., thirteen years United States Minister to China:* "In general, the tourists who spend a few days or weeks in China sneer at the missionaries, or damn them with faint praise. . . . Tourists who never put foot in a missionary compound have written books, nevertheless, teeming with criticism on the work of missions. I recall two prominent instances. One of the two was a distinguished American, who stayed three weeks in my legation. I particularly invited him to visit the missionary stations in Peking, but he declined to do so. He knew absolutely nothing of missionary work, but in his book he derided the whole system. The other gentleman was a celebrated Englishman, who has filled the highest offices under the Crown. He bitterly attacked the missionaries one day in conversation with me. I asked him if he had ever visited or inspected any missionary compound. He said he never had. . . . I do not believe that the tourist or the author treats the missionaries fairly. The world loves sensationalism, and an attack made on any established institution or any sentiment that humanity reveres, attracts much more attention than a calm, unimpassioned defense of the same establishments or ideas."

22. *William J. Bryan, journalist and traveler,* writing on his impression of India, says: "I do not apologize

for mentioning from time to time the institutions which altruistic Americans have scattered over the Orient. If we cannot boast that the sun never sets on American territory, we can find satisfaction in the fact that the sun never sets upon American philanthropy; if the boom of our cannon does not follow the orb of day in his daily round, the grateful thanks of those who have been the beneficiaries of American generosity form a chorus that encircles the globe."

IV

THE MISSIONARIES AND THE JOURNALIST
AND AUTHOR

WITH some notable exceptions, there is probably an impression in newspaper offices that the subject of foreign missions is generally unpopular. Until recently, missionaries have been classed by newspapers with inventors of perpetual motion and flying machines. The flying machine enthusiast is now in a position to command more respect than formerly, and no doubt the foreign missionary is not now so generally regarded as a person of impractical visions as he was a generation ago. The fact remains, nevertheless, that the ordinary space writer feels quite free to cast reflections upon the person, purpose, and methods of the foreign missionary, while not infrequently editorial writers draw learned conclusions from false premises condemning the entire foreign missionary purpose and effort.

It cannot be expected that men who are not themselves Christians will be in full sympathy with a movement that has for its aim the Christianization of all nations. Yet not infrequently even such men are impressed with the great good accomplished by medical, industrial, educational, and literary missions, while denying the value of the spiritual side of the work. They fail to see that all these various forms of work are but the fruits of the true spirit of Christianity in the hearts of the missionaries and of those who stand back of them. They do not understand that in order to make this work, which even they recognize to be beneficent, perpetually helpful to any people, it must be permeated with the spirit of true Christianity.

However much they may talk of the power of the press to make and change public opinion, there is no doubt that many editors carefully inquire as to what the people desire before declaring the policy of the paper. I am aware that this is a debatable and much debated question, and yet he is regarded a bold managing editor to-day who espouses a cause known to be unpopular. It can safely be assumed that, if an editor believes the great majority of his readers would prefer to see foreign missionaries ridiculed and their work adversely criticised, he will be slow to print much that is to their credit. When he does publish what seems to favor them, he is often quick to insert something that is critical, or a headline that is condemnatory, in order to save the paper. There are boundless illustrations where a statement of fact that was wholly creditable to the cause of missions was prefaced by headlines or editorial comment calculated to vitiate the value of the statement of fact following. Not infrequently a report of an address which is wholly commendatory to missions is distorted by the reporter, who acts upon the supposition that nothing wholly commendatory ought to be said.

In mission fields there are as yet few general newspapers. The missionaries have no complaint to make regarding the attitude of these papers as a whole to their work. Occasionally a newspaper correspondent makes a world tour, and at points comes in contact with mission work. Some of these correspondents have been fair-minded men who were not willing to accept as final the cheap gossip circulating about the lobbies of foreign hotels, but who sought out the missionaries and investigated for themselves the work done. To such men missions and missionaries owe a lasting debt of gratitude. These have represented journals that were ready to publish facts of every kind. Some of these reports have given helpful criticism which was of much value, while they have not withheld deserving approbation.

Some of the traveling newspaper men have gone abroad with the tacit, if not the written, understanding that a part of their commission was to " do up " missionaries. They knew at the start that no praise of missionary operations would be accepted at headquarters. Such as these have no difficulty in picking up, in any foreign country, stories that have been circulating for a generation or more, critical of missionaries and their work. But there is no doubt that the days of wholesale and indiscriminate criticism are passing. The missionaries have accomplished too much that is commendable to allow of universal condemnation.

Something of the same that has been said of newspaper correspondents may be said of authors. The author, for the most part, is attempting to make a book that will sell. It must, therefore, have the elements of popularity. If the writer is convinced that anything said favorable to missionaries will not meet with popular favor, unless he be a man of strength and independence, he will not say it, however much he may believe it. If he thinks an occasional slur or jibe at the missionaries will add to the popularity of his work, the chances are that he will occasionally indulge in that method of treatment. The approval or condemnation of missionaries by such authors has little or no real value.

It is to be expected that missionaries and their work will always be regarded by the space writer for so-called comic journals and for the joke columns of the secular press, as common plunder. Many interesting stories and ludicrous incidents have been created from imaginary missionary experience, and undoubtedly large numbers of those who heard or read them have obtained much enjoyment therefrom. To one that is familiar with missionary life and experiences, all these seem tame indeed when compared with the far larger and richer experiences of the men and women who, amid new languages, customs, and civilizations, constantly witness or experience that which is more ridiculous and astonishing. For genuine variety and ridiculous combinations and conditions, probably the life and experience of no class of people afford more. No one takes the comic journal seriously, and they do not expect so to be taken.

There are many other writers, honest and sincere men and women, some of whom have been prejudiced against missionaries, and who, upon close inspection, have been compelled to reverse their opinions. Many of these have spoken clearly and fearlessly of the things they have seen and do know. Their testimony is of value according to the extent and thoroughness of their investigation, and the fulness of their expression. There are a few—and they are few indeed—who are unable to see in mission work results that justify the cost. With probably no exception, these know little of what missions are accomplishing. For the most part they have little reliable information about any department or form of foreign missionary operations in any country. Missionaries and the officers of mission boards honor all such provided they are sincere and are ready to recognize well established facts when they appear. It would be most surprising if all who see missionary work should have the same opinions regarding it, or come to the same conclusion as to its relative efficiency and economy. All missionaries and missionary organizations desire to have the facts of the work widely published. They are desirous, however, that what is published shall be, not theories, or the conclusions of prejudice, or the repetition of exploded falsehoods, but the facts of missions which are always obtainable. During the last decade there have been many changes in the attitude of the so-called secular press toward the cause of foreign missions. These are recognizing that reports of the operations of foreign missionaries and the many institutions they have organized in foreign lands are regarded by the majority of their readers as news no less important than the gossip of European courts or the reports of the scientific explorer. In other words, the modern press is beginning to appreciate the news value of much that is accomplished through and by foreign missionaries.

ILLUSTRATIVE QUOTATIONS

1. *The "Japan Mail"* (October 18, 1892): "No single person has done so much [as the missionary] to bring foreigners and Japanese into close intercourse. His dictionary was the first book that gave access to the language of the country, and remains to this day the best available interpreter of that language. But even more than his dictionary has helped to facilitate mutual acquaintance, his life has assisted to break down the barriers of racial prejudice and distrust."

2. *Julian Hawthorne, author:* "The only salvation of India, even from an economic point of view, in the opinion of those who have longest and most deeply studied it, is its Christianization. Let England inspire India with a veritable Christian faith and nine-tenths of the present difficulties would spontaneously cease. One must live with the missionaries in India in order to understand what they are doing. . . . Their influences were of the loveliest Christian kind. There was no trace of that fanatic hunger for nominal converts which has often been ascribed to missionary work. I confess I had prepared myself to find something of the kind. I saw many native Christians. They were a remarkable and impressive body of men and women. I was always saying to myself, 'They are like the people of the Bible.'"

THE MISSIONARY AND HIS CRITICS

3. *Mark Twain (Samuel L. Clemens)*: "The benefit conferred upon this people [the Hawaiian Islanders] by the missionaries is so prominent, so palpable, and so unquestioned, that the frankest compliment I can pay them, and the best, is simply to point to the condition of the Sandwich Islands in Captain Cook's time, and their condition to-day. Their work speaks for itself."

4. *A London "Times" Correspondent, writing from China,* says of the missionaries: "They are the true pioneers of civilization. It is to them we have to look to carry the reputation of foreigners into the heart of the country; and it is on their wisdom, justice, and power of sympathy that the progress of China may largely depend."

5. *The "Forum"*: "There can be no doubt that while American commerce has been relatively declining in China, American missions have been relatively increasing. The factor of missions is to be reckoned with as much as the factor of trade. American missionaries have been free from the suspicion of acting as political allies; and they thus possess a decided advantage in attracting the natives to an honest acceptance of the Christian religion."

6. *Earnest W. Clement, newspaper correspondent and author:* "The missionaries have been, and are, a mighty force in New Japan, not merely through their preaching of the Gospel, but also through their practising of the Christian virtues; not only by their teaching of all-sided truth and wisdom, but also by their touching, their social contact with the people; not only by their logic but also by their lives. They are vivid and impressive object lessons of the ideal Christian life,—'living epistles,

74

known and read of all men.' They are, in general, well-educated men and women, a noble company, respected and loved by the Japanese. Christianity has already made an impression upon the commercial life of New Japan. The tremendous development of industry, trade, and commerce has required new business standards, and especially does it demand honesty and integrity. It is not infrequent, therefore, for companies and corporations to seek out young men trained in Christian schools, because they are most likely to be actuated by high ideals. The Sabbath, too, although Sunday is more a holiday than a holy day, is also proving to be a boon in business and labor circles, and is coming gradually to be observed more strictly. Christian socialism, too, is not without its influence in Japan. But there is a Christian head, because the leaders of New Japan are favorable to Christianity and its institutions, and are reconstructing the nation largely on Christian lines and with Christian ideals. And there is Christian life at the heart, for it is that life which is inspiring Japan with new ideas and ideals. And when we take into consideration how much Christianity has done for Japan in less than fifty years, we feel quite warranted in prophesying that within this twentieth century Japan will become practically a Christian nation."

7. *William Eleroy Curtis, correspondent and author:* "You frequently hear thoughtless people, who know nothing of the facts, but consider it fashionable to sneer at the missionaries, declare that Hindus never are converted. The official census of the government of India, which is based upon inquiries made directly of the individuals themselves, by sworn agents, and is not compiled from the reports of the missionary societies, shows an increase in the number of professing Christians from

2,036,000 in 1891 to 2,664,000 in 1901, a gain of 625,000, or thirty per cent. in ten years, and in some of the provinces it has been remarkable. In the Central Provinces and United Provinces the increase in the number of persons professing Christianity, according to the census, was more than three hundred per cent. In Assam, which is in the northeastern extremity of India, and the Punjab, which occupies a similar position in the northwest, the increase was nearly two hundred per cent. In Bengal, of which Calcutta is the chief city, the gain was nearly fifty per cent.; in the province of Bombay it was nearly forty per cent., and in Madras and Burmah it was twenty per cent.

"It is exceedingly gratifying to hear from all sides these and other similar encomiums of the American missionaries, and it makes a Yankee proud to see the respect that is felt for and paid to them. Lord Curzon, the governors of the various provinces, and other officials, are hearty in their commendation of American men and women and American methods, and especially for the services of our missionaries rendered during the recent famines and plagues. They testify that in all popular discontent and uprisings they have exerted a powerful influence for peace and order and for the support of the government.

"The medical and dispensary work of the American missions is also very extensive, and its importance to the peasant class and the blessings it confers upon the poor cannot be realized by those people who have never visited India and other countries of the East and seen the condition of women. As I told you in a previous chapter, ninety per cent. of the Hindu population of India will not admit men physicians to their homes to see women

76

patients, and the only relief that the wives, mothers, and daughters, and sisters in the zenanas can obtain when they are ill is from the old-fashioned herb doctors and charm mixers of the bazaars. Now American women physicians are scattered all over India healing the wounded and curing the sick."

8. *A. Michie, author of "Missionaries in China"*: "It is a gratifying fact which cannot be gainsaid, that Christians of the truest type—men ready to burn as martyrs, which is easy—and who lead helpful and honest lives, which is as hard as the ascent from Avernus— crown the labors of missionaries. It is thus shown that the Christian religion is not essentially unadapted to China, and that the Chinese character is susceptible to its regenerating power."

9. *Sir Edwin Arnold:* "I admire and reverence those devoted men and women [the missionaries], and I regard them as taking to China precisely the commodities of which she stands most in need, namely, a spiritual religion and a morality based on the fear of God and the love of man."

10. *W. F. Bainbridge, author:* "We have only a joyful report to render. There is encouragement all along the line. We cannot mistake the sun that shines at midday in a clear summer sky; we cannot mistake the evience that bathes the whole round world in its glowing light; that the age of universal missions on which we have entered will ultimately be crowned by the universal triumph of Christianity."

THE MISSIONARY AND HIS CRITICS

11. *Arthur T. Pierson, D.D., author, editor:* "Missions represent, not a human device, but a divine enterprise. The thought of missions was a divine idea, and the plan is a divine scheme; the work is a co-labor with God, the field is a divine inspiration and the fruit of missions is a divine zeal, an 'everlasting sign that shall not be cut off.'"

12. *Mr. Fukuzawa, Editor of the "Jiji Shimpo":* "If no missionaries had ever come to our country, the dissoluteness and wantonness of foreigners would have come to be much greater, and our relations to foreigners would not be what they now are.

"There can be no doubt that many serious troubles would have occurred had not the Christian missionary not only showed to the Japanese the altruistic side of the Occidental character, but also by his teaching and his preaching imparted a new and attractive aspect to the intercourse which otherwise would have been masterful and repellant. The Japanese cannot thank the missionary too much for the admirable leaven that he has introduced into their relation with foreigners."

13. *From the "Civil and Military Gazette" of India:* "No one can deny nowadays that the missionaries in India have done, and are doing, an immense amount of good work in practical fields apart altogether from their mission labors proper. During the course of the nineteenth century the linguistic labors of the missionaries have been extended far and wide, until there is hardly a nook or cranny of this great empire whose dialect has not been studied, and, in most cases, mastered, by devoted workers. The value of such labors cannot be overestimated."

78

14. *Boston "Daily Advertiser" upon the work of missons in Japan:* "Any attempt to estimate this thrillingly interesting phenonenon must fail through inadequacy that does not take largely into account the influence of Christian missions. They who do not know what they are talking about still say that missionaries have made no impression in heathendom except upon a relatively small fraction of the lower orders of mankind. They who speak from knowledge say that in Japan, to take that one case, Christian ideas have already permeated the institutions and populations of the country to such an extent that from the Mikado to the humblest laborer at four cents a day, there is no man in the island empire who does not directly or indirectly feel the influence of the new religion, if not as a spiritual force, at least as a creative energy in politics, industry, and learning. Statistics never can do more than dimly shadow forth the truth of such a matter. Yet statistics prove that already the faith of the missionaries has been accepted by thousands of joyful adherents, that the mission schools are educating tens of thousands of Japanese youth, that the missionary literature is scattered broadcast over that fertile field and that in all the native professions, in the ranks of the wealthy and powerful, and in all departments of the government, Christianity is deeply intrenched."

15. *Arthur L. Shumway, newspaper correspondent:* "Missionaries are, almost without an exception, men and women, not only of the most exalted Christian character, but also of the ripest scholarship and intellectual culture. Turn to the Oriental shelves in our libraries and you will be amazed to find that nearly all of the brightest, deepest, and most valuable books there have been written by mis-

sionaries. To missionary pens are we indebted for the most reliable information that we have regarding the Far East, as well as for the most fascinating, poetical, and scholarly of the correct pictures of Oriental life that we have. There are a few exceptions to this rule, but by their scarcity they only serve to prove the rule."

V

THE MISSIONARY AND FOREIGN RESIDENTS

FEW questions regarding missionaries are more puzzling to those who have never visited mission countries than the fact that so many American and European residents in foreign ports speak unfavorably of the missionaries and of their work. Not infrequently a foreigner residing at some Far Eastern capital writes an article for an English paper in which he speaks slightingly of the missionaries. Now and then some of these people return home and make unfavorable remarks. If the work done by the missionaries is as has been represented, and if they are men and women of the character they have been supposed to possess, how is it possible for those who have resided, it may be for years, in a city in which they are living and working, to have such an opinion regarding them? This is a natural and reasonable question upon which we will attempt to throw light.

Let us note at the beginning that not all English speaking residents in non-Christian countries speak against the missionaries and their work. Some of the strongest supporters and best friends of the missionaries are among these people. A long list of such as have given conspicuous testimony of the value of foreign missions and the high character of the missionaries might be given, did space permit. It is natural that we should persist in our inquiry as to how it is possible for one to reside for years in an Eastern city in which mission work is carried on, and not be compelled to acknowledge that it is a most valuable work. We will seek an explanation of the phenomenon.

In the first place many, if not most, of the foreign residents are not Christians and have no interest whatever in Christian matters. Many of them do not regard the Church of Christ anywhere in the world as of any value. They naturally class all missionaries as fanatical enthusiasts, without rhyme or reason in their religion and life, and they naturally affirm that the native religions are superior to Christianity, and that the missionaries only spoil the natives. They deprecate education for the native peoples, and often have much to say about the primitive simplicity and beauty of the lives and customs of the people before the missionaries spoiled them. Many of them openly maintain that education and Christian civilization belong exclusively to the white man, and that if the Lord had intended these advantages for Asiatic and African races, He would have created them of a different color.

With such men, there is no argument to use. They have no interest in Christianity, and much less in the men or women who take up their residence upon the other side of the earth to assist the native populations there to a genuine enlightened Christian civilization, and to plant among them institutions that will maintain it. The differences between these critics and the Christian missionaries are so great and fundamental that there is no common ground upon which to stand, except the commercial argument for missions, and no basis upon which discussion can be carried on. To be consistent, such as these are bound to sneer at missionaries, and, from their standpoint, foreign missionaries are about the most deluded mortals on earth.

There is another class of adverse critics among foreign residents in Eastern cities much more difficult to understand. It is painfully true that far too many excellent young men from England and the United States who go to the Far East in some secular pursuit, fall into evil company soon after their arrival. In some cities in the East, groups or clubs of young men are well known to have bound themselves together, and called to their aid the very devices of hell, in order to bring a newcomer down to their moral level. Many are caught unawares, and yield speedily to the temptations thrown in their way. Others who have come from Christian homes and an atmosphere of high morality, resist for a time, but finally yield. Others never yield. It is no wonder, in the face of these facts, that it should be a common saying among foreign residents, that when a young man leaves America or Europe for business residence among an Oriental people, he leaves his morals and his religion at home. This statement is not only common in every port in the East, but there is altogether too much truth in it.

Many men who at home moved in good society and were active members in a Christian church, are now living in some Eastern city in a manner that disgraces the name of our Christian civilization. Some native critics, seeing this, say, " Christianity will not endure exportation to the East." It cannot be expected that among such as these, who know no Sabbath, and who have abandoned, for the present at least, restraint against intemperance and impurity, there will be found any who do not hate the very name missionary because of the condemning conscience that the suggestion arouses in themselves.

As the writer was walking one of the main streets of a leading city in Japan with a foreign missionary, his attention was called to a finely dressed man coming down the other side of the street. The missionary said, " When we have passed on I will tell you about that man as an illustration of a missionary's not infrequent experience at an open port." It seems that some three or four years before, that man came to S—— and was there engaged in business. We will call his name, for convenience, Mr. A. Friends of Mr. A. in the home land wrote the missionary that he was at S——, giving account of his family, home surroundings, church connections, etc., and urged him to make the acquaintance of Mr. A. and try to get him interested in good things. The missionary at once looked him up and learned, at their first conversation, that Mr. A. had already got into a circle of acquaintances that would be of no help to him. Mr. A. talked very freely of the situation, and for a time endeavored, in a mild way, to break with his evil companions. He expressed great appreciation of the interest of the missionary, and frequently called at his house. This went on for a time, when the evil gained the ascendancy, and the young man openly espoused a life of shame. Once more the missionary went to him and pleaded, for the sake of the loved ones at home, if he was not willing to do it for his own sake, that he break from the evil and live an upright, pure life. Mr. A. finally said, " You have done for me all that an own father could do. You have fulfilled your whole Christian duty, and I honor you for it. I have deliberately chosen this life, with the companions it brings. I have left my religion at home, and do not intend to be bothered again with it until I return. You are the only one here who reminds me of it, and the reminiscence under these circumstances is most painful. I will therefore have to request you never to speak to me again upon this subject or upon any other subject. I have made the choice and intend to adhere to it. There is no use of saying anything more. I shall avoid you, and do not wish you to recognize me when we chance to meet. I shall not recognize you! Again thanking you for all you have attempted to do for me, I will bid you a final good-bye."

From that day to the time we met him, he had regarded the missionary as a stranger, and no sign of recognition had ever passed between them. His life was one of open shame. It is no wonder that he and all like him would prefer to have all Christian missionaries removed from the city in which they dwell. Their very presence, as well as the presence of Christian natives, is a constant reproach to them. Such men shun the presence or recognition of all Christians. As the Gadarenes who had taken up the profitable keeping of swine, in open violation of the Jewish law, besought our Lord and His disciples to depart from their coast, so these men hate the presence of those whose lives are a constant rebuke to them. From such let us look for no approval of missionaries or of their work.

We recall the conflict of the sailors with the missionaries in the early days of missionary work at Honolulu because, through their teachings, the native Christians refused to co-operate with them in carrying out their immoral purposes. The same violent opposition was created in the same way in the islands of the further Pacific. Men with immoral or dishonest purposes find themselves thwarted or rebuked through the presence of the missionaries, or by the developed moral sentiment of the natives. Christian men and Christian principles in any land discourage evil doers and tend to thwart them in the execution of their desires. Let not the Christian man hope for public approval from the man whose evil life his presence rebukes.

Many if not all of the commercial cities in the Far East cover a large area. There is usually a section of the city given up largely to the residence of foreigners, such as diplomats, consuls, and representatives of foreign business houses. In most cases the missionary lives in another section of the city, and in close touch with the native populations. It is in this way that he can do his best work. There is generally little relation existing between the foreign and native sections of the city. The work of the foreign missionary and the foreign official and merchant in an Eastern city are often almost as remote from each other as they would be if in different countries. The work of the missionary does not thrust itself upon the attention of the foreign residents. If they wish to see the missionary and his institutions, they must make preparations for it and look him up.

Some who lead upright lives, and are at heart interested in missionary operations, never get around to make the effort to investigate missions, and, after constant association with those who have no interest in Christian work, sometimes come to feel that maybe, after all, missions are a failure. After years of residence abroad, and after hearing from their associates little in favor and much against them, it is not surprising that they come home and sometimes give out that, after some years of residence in ——, they saw nothing of mission work, and heard little good of missionaries. This testimony is almost entirely negative, and, in most cases, if not in every case, would have been completely reversed had the person given a single day to personal investigation.

When the Hon. Alfred E. Buck was sent to Japan as United States Minister, although himself not a professing Christian, he decided that it was his official duty to become, as far as possible, personally acquainted with all resident Americans in Japan. The more he investigated, the more he became interested in the missionaries who comprised a good proportion of the American residents. At a diplomatic function in Tokyo which took place at about the time Mr. Buck had become well informed upon the work of American missionaries in Japan, the British Ambassador, in an address, made somewhat extended remarks about the incompetency and narrowness of missionaries. A little later Minister Buck was called upon to speak. He began by quoting the remarks of the British Ambassador derogatory to missionaries, and then added, " I assume that his excellency in his remarks about missionaries referred exclusively to British missionaries. I know positively that nothing he said applies to American missionaries, for I personally know most of them, and not a few have been guests in my house, and I have also been their guest, and I know whereof I speak." It later transpired that the British Ambassador knew practically nothing of his own missionaries, or of those of any other country. He had seen fit to voice a common criticism, supposing it would meet with popular favor in that audience. The gentle but unmistakable rebuke of the United States Minister was a wholesome surprise to all.

One reason why so many foreign ministers and consuls are able to speak so emphatically in favor of the missionaries and their work is that they have considered it their official duty to acquaint themselves with the operations of their own countrymen in the land to which they themselves were accredited, especially when, as in some countries, these represented the largest and most important national interest in the country. Some of the testimonials from diplomats and consular officials make this point clear.

We would not be understood as declaring that all foreign residents in Eastern cities who severely condemn the missionaries are immoral. Such a statement would be highly unjust. It can be stated, however, without fear of contradiction, that in every case when one of these residents has taken the trouble to acquaint himself with the missionaries, their institutions, purposes, and methods, he has voluntarily and openly spoken of that work as a whole in terms of unmistakable commendation.

There must necessarily be differences of judgment as to methods, proportions, and policies. One may think the missionary should do more in the line of education, another that the medical, industrial, or literary features should be emphasized, while some would omit all of them, and make the missionary only a preacher. Such criticisms as these will exist so long as men's judgments differ. Travelers and residents abroad who are careful observers can help the missionary work not a little by giving the missionary and the officers of the boards at home the benefit of their sympathetic criticisms. All welcome it.

Another source and method of general criticism should be noted. Now and then the best of mission boards will make a mistake in sending out a missionary who ought never to have gone. The mistake does not become apparent until he has been for some time upon the field. In that time he may have brought down upon himself and his colleagues much unfavorable criticism. No board desires to keep such representatives in any country. Every mission board desires to recall all missionaries who are not a positive help and a source of strength to the work. All such are recalled as soon as the facts can be ascertained. It is always better and far more Christian to communicate with the responsible board regarding an unworthy missionary than it is to indulge in general and sweeping remarks about the inferiority of missionaries as a whole.

Not infrequently self-appointed individuals, with zeal vastly in excess of intelligence or wisdom, secure independent support and go to some mission land to open a new work. These generally give little heed to what others have done or are doing, but proceed to propagate their own peculiar views in their own peculiar way. They are usually the most in evidence of any of the missionaries. They pose in public places, and conspicuously advertise themselves upon every available occasion. In some instances these constitute the only missionaries known to the foreign residents. It not infrequently happens that they take these irresponsible, irregular, untrained, and rattleheaded missionaries as a type of the fraternity as a whole. No greater injustice could be done to the foreign missionary cause. These people represent nothing, and are as severely condemned by the regular missionaries as by the outside critics. Many individual cases to illustrate this point might be cited.

When the writer was in Japan he was told by foreign residents and by leading Japanese that some of the missionaries in the empire were of no use, and were even injuring the cause and ought to be sent home. When the names of such useless missionaries were called for, invariably two irregular and untrained men were mentioned who were making themselves ridiculous before both Japanese and foreigners. They were there only a few years, but quite long enough to give to many the impression that foreign missionaries are rude, uncouth, fanatical fellows, whose main purpose seems to be to advertise themselves and make trouble for others. Every large mission country has such missionaries. It is not fair to judge regular missionaries and their work by this class, any more than it is to judge the medical profession by half-a-dozen quacks, or to condemn the entire United States Senate because one or two senators are unworthy.

All the missionary asks for his work is that it shall be judged upon its merits by those who understand it. All he asks for himself is that he may have an opportunity to meet his critics and answer in person their charges against him. Every missionary covets inspection, and delights in explaining that which is not understood.

It is not sufficient evidence of one's qualifications to criticise missionary work that he has resided for a time in a foreign port. That alone may constitute his chief disqualification. From such no sweeping condemnation should be accepted. One has a right to demand specific charges. In all such cases of criticism, the critic should be asked the name of individuals to whom he refers, and state the grounds of his knowledge. Such charges are too important to be made wholesale against a class of men and women who are held in such high esteem by the best people of Europe and America as are missionaries. Also the work they are doing as a whole has already received the commendation of too many people of unquestioned ability and sound judgment to be set aside as of no value, upon the general sweeping statement of anyone. The time has come when the one who would condemn missions or missionaries must make his charges definite, and substantiate them by reasonable evidence.

ILLUSTRATIVE QUOTATIONS

1. *Sir Bartle Frere, Governor of Bombay:* "Christianity has in the course of fifty years made its way to every part of the vast mass of Indian civilized humanity and is now an active, operative, aggressive power in every branch of social and political life on that continent.

"I speak simply as to matters of experience and observation, and not of opinion, just as a Roman prefect might have reported to Trajan or the Antonines, and I assure you that, whatever you may be told to the contrary, the teaching of Christianity among one hundred and sixty millions of civilized, industrious Hindus and Mohammedans in India is effecting changes, moral, social, and political, which, for extent and rapidity of effect, are far more extraordinary than anything you or your fathers have witnessed in modern Europe."

2. *Alfred Russel Wallace, scientist and author:* "The missionaries have much to be proud of in this country [the South Sea Islands]. They have assisted the government in changing a savage into a civilized community in a wonderfully short space of time. Forty years ago the country was a wilderness, the people naked savages, garnishing their rude houses with human heads.

Now it is a garden, worthy of its sweet name of 'Minahata.'"

3. *The Earl of Selborne, First Lord of the Admiralty, England:* "After eight years at the Colonial Office and Admiralty I have a profound contempt, which I have no desire to disguise, for those who sneer at missions."

4. *A British Nobleman, referring in a work on Bulgaria to the missionaries in that land:* "The result of their teaching has permeated all Bulgarian society, and is not the least important of the causes that have rendered the people capable of wisely using the freedom so suddenly conferred upon them."

5. *Archdeacon Thomas Spencer Childs:* "Whatever the future of these islands [Hawaiian], and I believe they have a magnificent future, the foundations of their greatness will rest on the work of the American missionaries."

6. *Henry E. O'Neill, British Consul at Mozambique:* "I must say that my experience of ten years in Africa has convinced me that mission work is one of the most powerful and useful instruments for the pacification of the country and the suppression of the slave-trade."

7. *Dr. John Dudgeon, thirty years resident in China, head of the Imperial College at Peking, and the physician and surgeon of the British and Japanese Legations in Peking:* "The missionary question of China is the question of the century. When you ask me if missionary enterprise in China has made for good, I answer, 'Unquestionably,' without reserve. Not only an almost unmixed good, but almost the only good. The civilization

that half the Powers would introduce is the civilization of selfishness. Railways are not everything and will not take the place of mental and moral training. We are upsetting the ideas of the Chinese and not giving them anything in their place. The only influence that can counteract the evil effects of breaking away from old restraints and abandonment of old beliefs is the civilization that springs from Christianity. It is the only hope of China."

8. *Sir H. O. Arnold-Forster:* "I do not believe Englishmen fully realize the enormous debt which Bulgaria owes to Dr. Washburn and Robert College. We see evidences of constitutional wisdom and an acquaintance with the principles and practice of free peoples at every turn in Bulgarian affairs; but we are at a loss to account for their existence in the little Eastern nation just struggling into life. The explanation is not far to seek. Nearly half the leading politicians in Bulgaria and Eastern Roumelia are old pupils of Robert College."

9. *Sir Charles Wood, Lord Palmerston:* "Independently of Christian consideration, we believe that every additional Christian in India is an additional bond of union with this country, and an additional source of strength to the empire. It is not only our duty, but it is our interest to promote the diffusion of Christianity as far as possible through the whole length and breadth of India."

10. *Hon. W. B. Reed, United States Commissioner:* "I went to the East with no enthusiasm as to missionary enterprise. I came back with the fixed conviction that missionaries are the great agents of civilization. I could

not have advanced one step in the discharge of my duties, could not have read, or written, or understood one word of correspondence on treaty stipulation but for the missionaries."

11. *Hon. James Bryce, M. P.,* says: " The longer one stays in India the more evidence one has that the future well-being of this country, and above all, the extension, permanence, and quality of British influence, depend largely upon the progress of missions."

12. *Commander A. V. Wadhams:* "It has been my privilege to see much of our missionaries and their work throughout the world. No one can fully appreciate the great good that has been done by foreign missionaries until he can compare the converted with the unconverted in distant lands and islands of the sea. The missionaries need no word of commendation from me or anybody. Their work speaks for itself; and any man or woman who honestly examines the work of our foreign missionaries must admire and rejoice in the great work that is being done by the noble men and women whose privilege it is to scatter the sunlight of the blessed Gospel."

13. *General Wagner, Austrian officer and drill master in the Persian army:* "Tell the church in America that I have seen the missionaries and have studied their work in Persia. I know about it. It is not a human work; it is angel work."

14. *The "Nation":* "Christian missions, as humanitarian institutions in India, have never come to the front as in these years of scarcity. Their praise is not only in the writings of Merewether and Hawthorne, but in the

mouths of English officials, who had ignored or despised them. No other whites except the missionaries are in touch with those whom the famine pinches most. No others are at all fit to be wardens of orphans more numerous than ever. No class can be so safely trusted as honest and wise almoners of bounty."

15. *The Hon. Charles Denby, LL. D., for thirteen years United States Minister to China:* "My acquaintance with the missionaries compels me to accord them high praise. In 1886 I personally visited nearly every missionary station on the seacoast of China, and some in the interior. I think I can testify as an impartial witness in their behalf. I came to the conclusion that the lives of the missionaries were pure; that they were devoted to their work; that they made many converts, and that these converts were morally, mentally, and spiritually benefited by their teachings. . . . It seems to be the general impression in this country that the missionary devotes all his time to purely religious work. He is attacked because he is charged with trying to force a new religion on the Chinese. There is not a people on the face of the earth which cares as little about religion as the Chinese. In general, the Chinaman has no religious belief. Confucianism is simply a philosophy. If the Chinese has any belief, it is merely pantheism, which by reason of its universality of deities so diffuses creeds that they become impalpable and general as the air. The average Chinese believes in nothing but the worship of ancestors, and that is mostly a matter of family pride. He wants a son to take care of his grave and do honour to his memory after he is dead. No other people are so tolerant, or, rather, so indifferent as to religious beliefs.

. . . It is not because of his religion that the missionary is attacked by mobs, it is because of his race. It is the foreigner, and not the Christian, against whom the mobs are gathered. The disturbances of 1900 have abundantly proved this to be true. . . . The missionary is always attacked because he is seeking to establish a new religion, but credit is never given to him for the good that he accomplishes. In fact, a great portion of the missionary's time is devoted to teaching, to healing the sick, to charity, and to literary work. . . . If the missionaries had done nothing else for China the amelioration of the condition of the women would be glory enough. . . . These, and other works of like character, are the doings of the missionaries. Will any tourist or author condemn them because they do these things? Will anybody deny that this teaching and charity are beneficial to the Chinese? If they are not, let us burn our schools, colleges, and hospitals. If the Chinese are benefited by these ministrations, it is certain that they react favorably on Western peoples,—but whether they do or not, why begrudge them to one-fifth of the human race? . . . There is scarcely anything finer in history than the defense of these two places, the British Legation and the Peitang. Let it be borne in mind that all this heroism occurred in one province and one city. The Province of Chihli furnished 6,200 people, who remained true to their faith in spite of danger, suffering, and impending death. It is said that fifteen thousand converts were killed during the riots, and not as many as two per cent. of them apostasized. I think that, in the face of these facts, the old allegation that the Chinese converts are treacherous, venal, and untrue, must be renounced. Let us not call them "rice Christians" any more. . . . Another objection made to mission work is that we are forcing a new civilization on China, and that her people are already civilized and have the right to maintain their ancient institutions. If there be any forcing, it is wrong, of course, but if by means of gentle persuasion we can introduce Western modes and methods into China, we are simply doing for her what has been done, in one way or another, for every nation on the globe.

"For nearly a century the missionary men and women have labored to carry our prestige, our language, and our commerce into China. They have borne every species of suffering, and they count many martyrs on their lists. The 'flowery flag' is known and respected in China. As our fellow citizens, and especially as self-sacrificing benefactors of humanity, the missionaries deserve our assistance and support. If we turn them adrift, our national fame will be dimmed. It cannot be doubted that by their disappearance our commerce would greatly suffer, and our diplomacy would lose its chief support.

"The labors of the missionaries, as has often been said, constitute some compensation to China for the wrongs that foreign association has entailed. When Sir Robert Hart was asked what was the prevention of anti-foreign riots, he said it was either partition or the conversion of China to Christianity."

VI

THE MISSIONARY AND HIS GOVERNMENT

IN most countries where missionaries have gone, they have preceded, often by a full generation, the representative of their government. The statement so often made—"The flag follows the missionary"—has much foundation in fact. The conclusion often drawn from the statement, namely, that the flag follows the missionary for his protection, is not generally true. Missionary work in the Hawaiian or Sandwich Islands was well established, and all fear for the personal safety of the missionaries or of their institutions long past, before the United States sent to the Islands an official representative. When the representative was accredited to that country, it was to foster the developing trade with the United States. It was after almost a generation of missionaries had passed away in the Turkish Empire, that a Minister was accredited to the Sublime Porte. The same is true, in a measure, of almost every missionary country in the world. Japan may seem an exception, but even here missionaries early in their work penetrated into the interior where no foreign consul was permitted to reside, and there remained unmolested.

To-day the foreign missionary is in Turkey, China,

Africa, and in the islands of the Pacific, as well as in other countries far remote from any official representative of his government. He is willing to continue to be, what he has been during the past century, the pioneer in foreign intercourse with strange and unknown peoples.

The fact that the missionaries have in so many cases been long residents of some countries before any representative of their government appeared, is sufficient evidence to show the superior knowledge of those countries and peoples which they must possess over the government representatives sent out. They have been sought after repeatedly as official interpreters, as secretaries of legations, as consuls, and even as ambassadors, because of their recognized ability to fill these positions. Occasionally, under pressure of some great urgency, a missionary has been persuaded to exchange his appointed task and work for the, to him, less congenial duties of the diplomatic corps, and several cases might be mentioned where such missionary diplomats have rendered most distinguished service to their country.

The much larger number, however, whose names have not come before the public, have declined the urgent call to this service, and have held to their missionary operations. There is a large, and perhaps a much larger class of missionaries who are the trusted advisers of the diplomatic representatives abroad. We all know how foreign offices are for the most part filled. Much has been said of the inefficiency of the American foreign diplomatic and consular service, owing to its political character and small salaries, together with the uncertain tenure of office. Men are frequently appointed, to say the least, not because of their special fitness for office. Such as these know little or nothing of the countries to which they are accredited, and even less of the questions they will have to consider in their official capacity. It is well known, by a few in the inner missionary circles, that ministers to foreign ports have frequently been instructed in Washington not to take any important step or act in any emergency without first consulting with some well-known local missionary. Cases are known in missionary circles where a legation interpreter has appeared before a veteran missionary bearing a troublesome official note written to the minister plenipotentiary, with the request from the minister that the missionary give the oral reply called for in answer to the note. The interpreter was ordered to take at once the reply to the proper authorities as the ministerial answer. Many times in the dead of night able and experienced missionaries have been hastily called to the legation to discuss some new emergency and advise as to necessary action.

These facts are not given by way of boasting, but to show that the superior knowledge necessarily possessed by the older missionaries is recognized by the home government and appreciated in multitudes of cases by the representatives abroad. The writer has been told by several such representatives that the advice given by missionaries had generally proved to be sound and free from personal prejudice. One said, " I never felt that it was safe to go against the advice of Mr. ——," a well-known missionary whom he consulted constantly.

This is no especial credit to the missionaries themselves. If these things were not true, it would constitute almost a reproach. They are as well educated as the official representatives, and usually much better; they have lived in the country long enough to become familiar with the spoken language of the people; and they have also made themselves conversant with the history, characteristics, and nature of the country and its government. It would be a reproach to a missionary board if, in these countries, a man could not be picked out at any time who would fill any diplomatic position with conspicuous credit to his country, should the place be offered him and could he be persuaded to accept it. This can be said with the greatest frankness, for no missionary of this class, except in the direst emergency, would consider for a moment giving up his missionary work for an official position.

This is declared in the face of the fact that now and then foreign Consuls, or Ministers, have spoken slightingly about missionaries and their work. We know full well that all missionaries have not the same ability and that now and then one gets into the work whose absence would strengthen rather than weaken his mission. But these are rare exceptions. We must at the same time remember that all Consuls and Ministers have not the same ability and that the diplomatic and consular service abroad would now and then be strengthened by the recall of some representatives.

MISSIONARY AND HIS GOVERNMENT

It requires no proof to show that many of our foreign representatives abroad have personally no interest in Christianity. They look upon the Christian as deluded, and one who goes abroad to propagate the delusion as a pure fanatic. In the eyes of such as these, the very fact that a man is a missionary condemns him as inferior in every way. He therefore tries and pronounces judgment upon the entire class unheard and uninvestigated. His evidence is taken from the traditional stories of foreigners and natives abroad who have no sympathy with Christianity in any land. Many of these stories have done service for a generation, and have been exploded many times, but to the man who has already condemned, or who is in search of justification for himself, they serve every purpose. I have never seen or heard a foreign minister or consul who condemned missionary work as a whole, or the missionaries as a class, who had proof for his position that would be acceptable in a court of justice. Such a man avoids the missionaries abroad, not giving them opportunity to exhibit their work and prove their position. He wishes no proofs, and seems to fear that to meet the missionaries and to see their work may endanger his pet theories regarding them, and this, above all things else, he wishes to avoid.

There is another side to the picture that is turned with hesitation, but which should be shown in order to the fullest understanding of the subject. It is well known, and nowhere better than in London and Washington, that now and then unworthy men are sent abroad to fill official positions. The writer was taken one day in a foreign city to call upon the United States Minister. It was a notorious fact in that city, among representatives of other governments as well as among our own citizens, that there were frequently periods of long duration when the business of the United States Legation had to be transacted by a secretary, because the Minister was in no condition to do business. His dissolute life was known to the entire community, and was a constant reproach to the nation he represented. In response to an inquiry, the missionary in that place said that he had never written a word about the character of the man, and that he was doing all he could to hide the disgrace. It is not strange that this man said, after his recall, that missionaries were doing no good in ——. Cases could be cited, if there could be any gain in making such citation, where missionaries have attended official representatives of the United States when they were prostrated by unseemly debauches, who, after being brought safely through, seemed to feel intolerably bitter towards the very men who had saved them from great shame, if not severe sickness. It seemed to gall them that a fellow citizen, and he a missionary, should know of their disgrace. Some of this class cannot say enough against the missionaries, and seem to delight in condemning that in which their own lives have no part or interest.

This is not indiscriminate condemnation of foreign official representatives. Among the foreign diplomats and consuls in mission lands are some of the best men to be found anywhere. Nor do we wish to be understood as even suggesting that all those who condemn missionaries and their work are unworthy men. Such a statement would be an injustice of itself. It is true, however, that so far as known to the writer, no foreign Minister or Consul who has taken the pains to look into missionary work and to become acquainted with the missionaries, has failed to commend them. Some of those who have been among the most profuse in their commendations have not been professing Christians themselves. They have praised that which they saw to be beneficial to the people of the country so far as this present life is concerned, without reference to the religious character of the work done.

There is no conflict between the missionary and the resident Consul and diplomat. The non-Christian man will not feel drawn to the man and the work that is supremely Christian; and the vicious man will naturally shun, if not openly hate, the man whose very profession and life condemn his own. At the same time, the broad-minded, large-hearted men who represent us in the mission field do not allow prejudice to prevent them from becoming personally acquainted with all foreign enterprises in their fields, and they do not hesitate to approve that which is worthy of approval, and condemn that which is worthy of condemnation.

It has been occasionally said in political debates and by men hostile to the missionary enterprise, that the principal reason for sending abroad ministers and consuls is to protect the missionaries and their work. This statement has so little fact upon which to rest that the truth should be known. There is no question whatever that when the true history of diplomacy in the mission lands is written, it will appear that the missionaries have rendered far more service to the government representatives abroad than they ever demanded from them. Apart from Turkey and China, rarely have the missionaries appealed to consular or diplomatic agents for assistance, and in these cases such appeals have not been as frequent as we might imagine.

In no case have missionaries asked for or received government aid in the propagation of missionary operations. Reference is now made only to Protestant missionaries. Many of the political methods employed by the European Catholic missionaries have been charged against all who bear the name missionary. A greater injustice to Protestant missions in the East could hardly be rendered. Protestant missionaries have not sought for or obtained special privileges as missionaries. They have not asked the aid of their governments in any form for the propagation of mission work as such. They have unfailingly obeyed the laws of the countries to which they have been sent, and have been most scrupulous in planning their work so that it shall be fully covered by the treaties, precedents, and capitulations between those countries and their own.

These treaties and capitulations were not devised especially to cover missionary operations, but to cover the relations of foreign citizens and their property in those countries. It must not be assumed for a moment that a missionary, by accepting missionary appointment, loses his identity or rights as a citizen. Most of the false reasoning upon this matter arises from the false premise that "a missionary has no rights which an individual or a foreign government is bound to respect." This is not the reasoning of the governments at Washington, London, and Berlin, but it is the line of argument many employ who seek for proof that the missionary is a troubler of the otherwise placid waters of international diplomacy. Treaties between Western governments and China, Japan, Turkey, and other countries in which missionaries are at work, were made primarily for the trader, the merchant, and the traveler. It would be difficult to find a single section of a single treaty made for the benefit of the missionaries. The writer is not aware that mission boards of America or Europe have ever asked that special treaties be made, or special clauses inserted in existing treaties to aid them in the propagation of missionary work. Neither missionaries nor missionary boards believe that Christianity can be wisely propagated or Christian institutions permanently established in any country by force. The Gospel of Jesus Christ is a gospel of love and peace, and the sentiment of every missionary society in the world would be arrayed against measures that would employ the army or the navy to compel any country to accept missionaries or their institutions.

We must not lose sight of the fact, however, that every missionary anywhere in the world is a citizen of his native land. By accepting appointment as a missionary he no more loses or forfeits his citizenship than does the clergyman, teacher, or physician who remains at home, or the merchant or traveler who goes abroad. No civilized country has a law or custom by which men entering certain professions shall thereby cease to be citizens, or that certain men and women, law-abiding citizens at home, shall be deprived of that citizenship when they go abroad. No nation has such a custom of class or professional distinction, nor would any people tolerate such a discrimination. Every law abiding, native-born citizen remains a citizen, whatever his profession, and wherever his residence, until he chooses to renounce such citizenship. As a citizen, every right and privilege belonging to such belongs to him and must be accorded him. More than this, it is the duty of his government to see that his just rights as a citizen are accorded him; for, if any country is to obtain for any of its citizens in any part of the world all of the rights and privileges that belong to them, it must insist that these same rights and privileges are granted to all its citizens. Foreign missionaries could take no step that would give their respective governments more trouble than to insist that, for themselves, they will forego some or all of the rights that belong to citizens residing in the countries where they live. The lawless hordes which recognize the missionary and the merchant and traveler as foreign, would be slow to understand why the liberties taken with the one class could not be taken with all. In the eyes of the native populations, if not of the officials of Asiatic countries, the protection of a

Western power over its citizens is measured by its strength at its weakest point. A government which does not protect all of its citizens, all of the time, is impotent, in their judgment, and can be defied with impunity. For the sake of all foreigners abroad, it is imperative that missionaries receive the same protection as others, and that personal injury done the missionary, be treated by your government the same as though the case were that of an ordinary tourist or merchant.

It goes without saying, that the missionary, as the merchant or traveler, is bound to abide by the laws of the country in which he is a guest and not to overreach the treaties, capitulations and precedents relating to foreigners residing in those respective countries or traveling through them. Any missionary who violates the laws of the country where he is at work, or the treaties existing between that country and his own, should meet the penalty of such violation the same as any other citizen. While his profession imposes upon him no political disabilities, it affords him no immunities. He is a foreigner residing abroad, entitled to all the rights and privileges accorded by law to foreigners in that country and subject at the same time to all their limitations.

What has been said regarding the person of the missionary is equally true of the funds invested by him in the prosecution of his legitimate missionary work. The house that he has purchased or erected for himself, the land upon which it stands, the buildings for colleges, schools, churches, hospitals, dispensaries, asylums and printing plants, all purchased or erected in accordance with the laws of the land, and the treaties and capitulations covering the holding of property in these countries by foreigners, constitute foreign property as much as the houses of merchants and their agents, or the warehouses in which they store their goods. As such, they are not only entitled to full protection, but they must be protected for the sake of all foreign interests in those countries. The same reason for this protection prevails which operates in the protection of the person of the missionary. If it should come to be understood that mission property can be injured or destroyed without fear of retribution, it would at once be interpreted that the government is too weak to protect the property of its citizens, and all foreign property would be jeopardized. It would not help matters politically for the missionaries to maintain that they wish no protection. If all missionaries and all mission boards should take this ground, it could not be, and certainly would not be, respected by the governments, which must either protect all the property of all its subjects or attempt to protect none. When a missionary's residence is wantonly destroyed, or a mission college pulled down by a mob, the home government, acting through its proper representative, does not ask the missionary if he wishes indemnity for his loss, but demands a statement of the facts of the case and an account of the losses incurred. The question is not a missionary question, but it becomes at once a question of the protection of foreign interests in that country and whatever measures are necessary to accomplish this are taken by the government. The same is true when a missionary is treated with indignity or is killed; it ceases at once to be a missionary question and becomes a question of citizenship. Neither the missionary nor his colleagues are asked whether protection is desired, but measures for proper protection are at once taken and indemnity is demanded and collected, because this is necessary for the protection of all foreigners in that country.

It is well understood that it is in the province of the representative of a government in any country, when he is convinced that proper protection cannot be afforded its citizens or their property in any particular place at that time, to inform them of the conditions and tell them that if they wish or expect government protection they must withdraw from the danger zone. Whoever fails to withdraw, after receiving such notice, remains at his own peril. It is the duty of every government to warn its citizens in all such cases, but at the same time, the subject, whatever his profession or occupation, has the right to assume the responsibility and stay where he is, or even to enter dangerous districts. A government cannot be expected to secure redress for indignities suffered by subjects thus acting. Probably, under such circumstances, missionaries have ignored these warnings and remained at their posts, more generally than any other class of citizens. In but a few cases have they suffered by it. Such an act has not been a defiance of their relations as citizens to their officials abroad, nor has it ever been so interpreted by State Departments, but it has been a personal assumption, upon the part of the missionary, of all risks, because, in his judgment, the interests of the missionary work and the safety of the native Christians demanded his continual presence at that point. Travelers, especially explorers and scientific investigators, have often done the same thing in the interests of science, and merchants have occasionally done it in the interests of gain.

There can be but one conclusion to this dsicussion, and that is that the missionary is entitled to and should receive the same personal protection in foreign countries that is accorded travelers, merchants, and traders, and that his institutions and supplies must have the same protection that his government gives to the homes and institutions of the merchant and trader. A foreign college in Turkey or in China has the same right to protection as the kerosene warehouse or the whisky depot, and an invoice of Western Bibles is as legitimate a line of goods as Connecticut clocks, New England rum, or British opium.

The sooner we cease to think of the foreign missionary as a separate and distinct class by himself, and his work as exceptional, the sooner will we have a clear understanding of him in relation to all other world operations.

missionary effort is that which regards it, not like a prairie fire that sweeps rapidly over the plains, devouring all within its range, and so swiftly dying out; but, rather, as a mighty, silent influence, like the quiet, steady forces of nature, which carry the seed and deposit it in the soil, nursing it with sunshine and with rain year after year until an oak springs up and reaches out its growing arms over the sod, and in time scatters the acorns, until a mighty forest waves its majestic boughs where once were rocks and thistles. Ages passed while nature was producing this great evolution; and they who judged superficially by the few acorns first produced might have sneered at the slow but sure results that were to come after they had mouldered in the grave. Men do not reason about other great movements as they do about missions. Is it fair, is it just, is it sensible to make an exception in this case? American missions in Persia may be seemingly slow, but they are an enduring influence both for secular as well as for religious progress. Their growth is culminative and their power is mighty."

2. *Colonel Alfred E. Buck, United States Minister to Japan:* "The influence of the missionaries has been worth more to Japan than all other foreign influence combined."

3. *Hon. John Barrett, journalist and United States Minister and Consul-General to Siam:* "From careful study of the scope of missionary labor, not only in Siam but in China and Japan, during a period of nearly six years, I am convinced beyond question that the missionaries are doing a great and good work for the advancement of both the moral and material interests of these Asiatic lands.

" The explanation of much of the anti-missionary talk is found in the superficial gossip of the treaty ports of Asia. It is the tendency in the clubs of Yokohama, Tientsin, Shanghai, Hong Kong, and Bangkok, to speak lightly of the missionaries and the fruits of their endeavors, without serious knowledge of what is really being done, and of the progress that is made along educational, medical, and evangelical lines. The average traveler hears this talk, and goes away with a prejudiced opinion. On the other hand, those who study carefully the work of the missionaries, not only in the treaty ports, but in the interior, and weigh carefully in the balance all adverse and all favorable conditions, agree that the missionary field should not be limited but rather extended."

4. *Hon. John Goodnow, United States Consul-General to Shanghai, China:* " Our missionary enterprises, hospitals, schools, and churches have won for us the good will of the Chinese people. All the institutions of Western learning for Chinese are American and missionary. One cannot overestimate their influence. I know of one hospital that last year treated 33,000 cases of women and children free. That hospital is only one of many doing a similar work of noble charity. Before I went to China I had my misgivings as to adult Chinamen ever becoming true converts to Christianity, but when the time of trial came, last year, [1900] and tens of thousands of Chinese in the North refused to recant their Christian professions, but sacrificed their lives, martyrlike, on the block, they gave a supreme test to their belief in the Savior of mankind.

" The thing that makes us more popular in China is the work of our missionaries. The fact that the American nation and the American people stand in better relations toward the Chinese nation and people is due almost wholly to these facts: First, the work of the missionaries proper, by preaching the word; second, the splendid work of the medical missionaries with their hospital service where thousands upon thousands of poor natives are treated and cared for; thirdly, to the fact, commonly recognized by the Chinese of intelligence, that the Americans and the American people do not want Chinese territory."

5. *Hon. Hamilton King, United States Consul-General to Siam:* "In this field the influence of Christian civilization, divorced to a very large degree from those evils that generally go hand in hand with it, have been brought to bear upon the Oriental mind through the agency of the Christian mission alone. As we approached the city of Chiengmai, where the work has been longest in operation, it was interesting to mark the external evidences of improvement that greeted us. Each day the women that we met were more neat and trim in appearance: their faces wore a more hopeful look, and they bore the mark of better things in their lives. The roads became better: better tilled fields, better kept fences, better houses, more thrifty homes, and a general improvement in all that goes to make up a prosperous and thrifty people were evident in this province. On the morning after my arrival, as I stood before an audience of 600 people in the commodious church, I said to myself, 'This is the best thing I have seen in Siam.'"

6. *Hon. George F. Seward, United States Minister to China:* "During my twenty-years' stay in China I always congratulated myself on the fact that the mis-

sionaries were there. There were good men and able men among the merchants and officials, but it was the missionary who exhibited the foreigner in benevolent work, as having other aims than those which may justly be called selfish. The good done by missionaries in the way of education, of medical relief, and of other charities cannot be overestimated. If in China there were none other than missionary influences, the upbuilding of that great people would go forward securely. I have the profoundest admiration for the missionary as I have known him in China. He is a power for good and peace, not for evil."

7. *The Seventh Earl of Shaftesbury:* "I do not believe that in the whole history of missions—I do not believe that in the history of diplomacy or in the history of any negotiations carried on between man and man, we can find anything to equal the wisdom, the soundness, and the pure evangelical truth of the body of men who constitute the American Mission. I have said it twenty times before, and I will say it again—for the expression appropriately conveys my meaning—that they are a marvellous combination of common sense and piety. Every man who comes in contact with these missionaries speaks in praise of them. Persons in authority and persons in subjection all speak in their favor. Travelers speak well of them, and I know of no man who has ever been able to bring against that body a single valid objection. There they stand, tested by years, tried by their works, and exemplified by their fruits: and I believe it will be found that these American missionaries have done more toward upholding the truth and spreading the Gospel of Christ in the East than any other body of men in this or any other age."

8. *General Lew Wallace, United States Minister to Turkey:* "I have often been asked, 'What of the missionaries of the East? Are they true, and do they serve their Master?' And I have always been a swift witness to say, and I say it solemnly and emphatically, that if anywhere on the face of the earth there exists a band of devout Christian men and women, it is these. They live and die in the work. Their work is of that kind which will be productive of the greatest good."

9. *Hon. E. F. Noyes, United States Minister to Turkey:* "The salutary influence of American missionaries and teachers in the Turkish Empire cannot possibly be overrated. By actual observation I know that wherever a conspicuously intelligent and enterprising man or woman is found in the East, one imbued with the spirit of modern civilization, it is always found that he or she was educated in an American college. With the educational influences comes a demand for the refinement of civilized life."

10. *Mr. Medhurst, British Consul at Shanghai, China:* "I have no sympathy with those, who, for want of consideration or from prejudice, think lightly of the work and character of the missionary. I am only doing them simple justice when I state that their efforts have been attended with exceptional success."

11. *Minister Buck, quoted by Edward Abbott, D. D.:* "The strongest testimonies for missions come, not from missionaries, theorists, or hurrying travelers, but from foreign residents in non-Christian lands, who know whereof they speak, and from the natives for whom Christian missions have been an introduction to a new life. As one example of such testimonies—and their

117

name is legion—I will simply quote *the late Mr. Buck, United States Minister to Japan,* who told me with his own lips, in 1901, as I sat with him in a Christian parlor in the city of Tokyo, that the result of his years of observation in that country was that Christian missions had done more for the advancement of the Japanese people than all other influences and forces put together."

12. *Colonel Charles Denby, United States Minister to China:* "I have made it my business to visit every mission in the open ports of China. This inspection has satisfied me that the missionaries deserve all possible respect, encouragement, and consideration. I find no fault with them except excessive zeal. Civilization owes them a vast debt. They have been the educators, physicians, and almoners of the Chinese. They are the early and only translators, interpreters and writers of the Chinese. To them we owe our dictionaries, histories, and translations of Chinese works. They have scattered the Bible broadcast, and have prepared many schoolbooks in Chinese. Commerce and civilization follow where these unselfish pioneers have blazed the way. Believe nobody when he sneers at the missionaries. The man is simply not posted on the work.

"I have made a study of missionary work in China. On a man-of-war I visited almost every open port in China. At each place I inspected every missionary station. I saw the missionaries in their homes. They are doing good work and merit all the support that philanthropy can give them. I do not stint my commendation. I unqualifiedly and in the strongest language that tongue can utter, give to these men and women who are living and dying in China and in the Far East my full and unadulterated commendation."

MISSIONARY AND HIS GOVERNMENT

13. *Mr. J. P. Donovan, British officer in China:*
"Many of our countrymen in China are too indifferent to inquire or examine for themselves the work that is being done, and the character and conduct of others is such that they studiously avoid missionaries. But, those who will take the trouble to go and see, soon discover a great work. I have seen it myself in Shanghai, Tientsin, Hankow, and Peking, and can speak of it from personal knowledge and observation. Indeed, the ignorance of Christian people at home about this great work amazes me."

14. *Hon. S. G. W. Benjamin, United States Minister to Persia:* "The American missionaries have now been laboring fifty years in Persia. There are captious persons who ask, 'Well, how many converts have they made? Would they not do more by staying at home?' Although this is not a fair way to judge of the value and results of missions, I have no hesitation in affirming that the missionaries in Persia have made as many converts as an equal number of clergymen in the United States during the same period. American missions in Persia may be slow, but they are an enduring influence both for secular as well as for religious progress. Their growth is cumulative and their power is mighty."

15. *John W. Foster, Secretary of State and diplomat:* "Much diversity of sentiment has been expressed by writers upon the effects of the labors of the Christian missionaries in the Orient, but the better judgment of candid observers is in favor of their beneficial influence on the rulers and the people, even aside from the religious considerations involved. Their useful service in con-

nection with the diplomatic intercourse of the Western nations with the far East has been especially conspicuous.

"I have a high estimate of the Chinese race. As we study their history and recall their achievements in the past four thousand years, we can hardly wonder at their spirit of exclusiveness and conceit. When once the barriers of official conservatism are removed and the people are free to receive the Gospel, I have great faith that large success will attend the missions. The accession of the Chinese race, or a considerable portion of it, to Christianity will be a great achievement, and will materially change the history of mankind."

16. *Captain Thomas Catesby Jones, who negotiated and signed the first formal treaty entered into by the Hawaiian Islands with the United States, in his report says:* "Not one jot or tittle, not one iota derogatory to their character as men, or ministers of the Gospel of the strictest order, or as missionaries, could be made to appear by the united efforts of all who conspire against them."

17. *Hon. David B. Sickles, United States Consul at Bangkok, Siam:* "The American missionaries in Siam, whom I have observed for several years, have accomplished a work of greater magnitude and importance than can be realized by those who are not familiar with its character, and with the influence which they have exerted upon the Government and people. Largely through their influence slavery is being abolished, and the degrading custom of bodily prostration is not compulsory. Wholesome and equitable laws have been proclaimed, criminals have been punished by civilized methods, literature and art have been encouraged by the king and ministers, an educational institution has been established by the gov-

ernment, and reforms have been inaugurated in all its departments. Before I went to the Far East I was strongly prejudiced against the missionary enterprise and against foreign missionaries: but after a careful examination of their work, I became convinced of its immense value."

18. *Hon. Lloyd C. Griscom, United States Minister to Japan and formerly connected with United States legations at Constantinople and in Persia:* "My views are entitled to the greater weight inasmuch as prior to my being sent abroad as representative of the Government, first to Turkey, and afterwards to Persia, I had not been in sympathy with missionary work: was, perhaps, hostile and inclined to ridicule the work of foreign missions. The change wrought in my views was due to my having been brought into close intimacy with what missionaries were doing, as in Turkey, and at Teheran, and at Ispahan in Persia. At the former was a single lady, an M. D., surrounded by 30,000 hostile Mussulmans. At Ispahan a whole colony of English and Americans were giving themselves to the education and betterment of the people. I can hardly express my admiration for the self-sacrifice exhibited."

19. *Hon. Benjamin Harrison, President of the United States:* "The enemies of foreign missions have spoken tauntingly of the slowness of the work and of its great and disproportionate cost, and we have too exclusively consoled ourselves and answered the criticism by the suggestion that with God a thousand years are as one day. We should not lose sight of the other side of that truth —one day with Him is as a thousand years. God has not set a uniform pace for Himself in the work of bring-

ing in the Kingdom of His Son. He will hasten it in His day. The stride of His Church shall be so quickened that commerce will be the laggard. Love shall outrun greed."

20. *The Marquis of Salisbury:* "I firmly believe that, on the whole, the missionaries have been a great power for good in China. . . . I would rather have all their rashness than not have them at all. Would that we at home could catch a spark of their zeal!"

21. *Major Edwin H. Conger, United States Minister to China and Mexico:* "For seven years I have been intimately associated with your colleagues in the missionary work in China, a body of men and women who, measured by the sacrifices they make, the trials they endure, and the risks they take, are veritable heroes. They are the pioneers in all that country. They are invariably the forerunners of Western civilization. It is they, who, armed with the Bible and schoolbooks, and sustained by a faith which gives them unflinching courage, have penetrated the darkest interior of that great empire, hitherto unvisited by foreigners, and blazed the way for the oncoming commerce which everywhere quickly follows them. It was they who first planted the banner of the Prince of Peace in every place where now floats the flag of commerce and trade. The dim pathways which they traced, sometimes marking them with their life's blood, are rapidly being transformed into great highways of travel and trade, and are fast becoming lined with schoolhouses and railway stations, where heretofore were found only idolatrous shrines and lodging houses for wheelbarrow men and pack mules. Hundreds of splendid schools have been founded, and are now being most

successfully taught by these good men and women, and it is a fact in which we may all take great pride, that ninety-five per cent. of the Protestant schools in China have been established by Americans."

22. *George, King of Great Britain, Letter to Bartholomew Ziegenbalg and John Ernest Gundler of Tranquebar:* " Reverend and beloved: Your letters dated the 20th of January of the present year were most welcome to us, not only because the work undertaken by you, of converting the heathen to the Christian truth, doth, by the grace of God, prosper; but also because that in this, our kingdom, such a laudable zeal for the promotion of the gospel prevails."

23. *King Edward VII., when in India, as Prince of Wales, in 1895, said to a deputation of missionaries and native Christians,* " It is a great satisfaction to me to find my countrymen engaged in offering to our Indian fellow-subjects those truths which form the foundation of our own social and political system, and which we ourselves esteem as our most valued possession."

24. *President Theodore Roosevelt, at the Ecumenical Missionary Conference in 1900, said:* " You are all doing the greatest work that can be done. It is an honor and a privilege to greet you here to-night in the name of the great State of New York, which includes within its borders the greatest city of the western hemisphere. I greet you in the name of the people and of the State: I bid you welcome, and I extend to you who lead hard and dangerous lives, you who have given up so much that most deem attractive in life, to you who have sacrificed so much that most hold dear, I give to you no commiseration, no sympathy, but the heartiest homage, the heartiest

admiration and good will. . . . I wish it were in my power to convey my experience to those people —often well-meaning people—who speak about the inefficacy of foreign missions. I think if they really could realize but a tenth part of the work that is being done and the work that has been done, they would realize that no more practical work, no work more productive of fruit for civilization could exist than that work being carried on by men and women who give their lives to preach the Gospel of Christ to mankind—the men and women who not only have preached but have done; have made action follow pledge, performance square with promise."

25. *The Hon. Chester Holcombe, diplomat and author:* " The missionary possesses only such privileges, exemptions, and immunities under treaty, as are granted to his fellow alien of every other class and occupation. The right to reside, acquire property, and to pursue his calling at certain specified centers of population, mostly upon the sea-coast, and to travel freely under passport, throughout the interior, covers all to which he is entitled under the official pledge and seal of the government of China.

" In a nation where popular opinion and sentiment to an almost unprecedented extent guide and limit governmental policy,—for all the nominally autocratic authority of the Emperor,—the presence of such a force at work quietly among the people is of the utmost value in the establishment and maintenance of good relations and the development to their full limit of all mutual interests. No other foreigner comes in such close and intimate touch with the native as he. And he is the unrecognized and uncommissioned representative of what is best in every phase and department of American life."

VII

THE MISSIONARY AND LOCAL OFFICIALS

IN many respects a supreme test of the value of missionary operations, is the opinions regarding them, held by the rulers of the country in which they are at work. This must necessarily be a severe test, because in many, if not in the great majority of cases, these men have no sympathy with Christianity. This being the case, they must necessarily be prejudiced against the men and women who leave their homes to Christianize the natives and introduce among them the institutions of Christianity.

Another reason, perhaps more fundamental than the one already given, why rulers of a country, especially if they be foreign rulers as in India and Ceylon, South Africa, etc., are at first opposed to missionaries and their work, is that they are liable not to be in sympathy with any effort which tends to exalt the natives and lift them in the social or intellectual scale. To many of these people the " native " is little if any better than the beast, and to make him think he is anything looks like a colossal mistake from the governmental standpoint. The " Ethiopian Question," which is now disturbing the government of South Africa, arises in no small measure from the education, advancement and ambitions of the Zulus. Any government that depends for its success upon maintaining a low degree of intelligence among the native races, cannot look with favor upon the missionary who believes that the native is a man, that he has within him possibilities of moral, intellectual and physical advancement. Now and then such a ruler calls the missionaries disturbers of the regular order of things, introducers of vexatious and trying questions and even propagators of revolutionary ideas.

There can be no question that not a few of the results of missions are revolutionary in character. A native race that has existed hitherto in entire ignorance of letters or a written language, that has no education except tradition and experience, cannot be taught to read its own language and through it study modern science, history, geography and religion, without passing through something of a revolution. If to this is added instruction in Christianity so that old heathen customs are laid aside, and, in their place, are adopted customs that harmonize with those of Christian society, and if the outward life takes on the forms and habits of self-respecting, enlightened and civilized society, we need no further proof to show that a mighty revolution has been at work among that people. These changes are taking place in a greater or less degree in many of the foreign mission fields of the world. Heathen society and most of the customs prevailing among pagan races must be changed in order to tally with the demands of Christian society and modern Christian civilization. Whoever is opposed to such changes, either for political, commercial or other reasons, must be hostile to the presence of the missionary who is there to produce precisely those results.

Perhaps one of the best illustrations of such hostility to missionary operations is that displayed by the Sultan of Turkey. His method of administering the government is such that political affairs operate with the least friction among an ignorant and unthinking people. From the standpoint of the Sultan, the best citizen is one who never thinks for himself and who has no conception of personal rights or justice beyond what his government affords him. The perfectly loyal Turkish subject must accept whatever is as from God without question or complaint. It requires no demonstration to prove that under such a method of government, especially when it is shot through and through with injustice and open abuse, modern mission colleges and an extensive system of education for the masses, are not acceptable and never can be, until government methods radically change.

In South Africa, as long as the English rulers stand in fear of the educated Zulu and feel called upon to hedge him about with unjust regulations and unreasonable taxation, in order to prevent his rising in the scale of civilization, there cannot fail to be trouble for the government officials, the missionaries and the governed.

The present governor of Natal, South Africa, has organized his government upon a plan to suppress ambition in the native population of the country, to keep them in subjection and poverty, and to prevent them from having any part in the affairs of state. So long as the people remained in gross ignorance the task was not a difficult one. Mission schools and the development of native talent along lines of independence and leadership, together with native churches presided over by trained Zulu pastors, have not met with the approval of the administration. This government policy demands white superintendence of all colored schools and congregations, and anything less than this fosters, in his judgment, undue native supremacy. Such a policy of suppression can best be carried on without the presence of missionary institutions. It is not, however, a policy that commends itself to the civilized world.

On the other hand, in India and Ceylon, where the two governments are eager for more and better trained natives to take places of responsibility and trust, and where the trades and professions are calling for educated and trustworthy natives to organize and direct large and needed enterprises, the missionary not only finds a warm welcome, but the governments are ready to subsidize his schools and to give him every encouragement possible in his efforts for general education and industrial training.

The missionaries have never failed to have a warm welcome in Japan ever since her doors were thrown wide open to modern education. The same cannot fail to be true in China now that the country is beginning to admit modern science and is recognizing its superiority over the old classics in the curriculum of her school system.

King Leopold, who is now directing with a high

hand the affairs of the Congo " Free " State in Africa, is opposed to the presence of missionaries for the same reason that the Sultan of Turkey wished them out of his country at the time of the notorious Armenian massacres in 1894 and 1895. In both cases the missionaries have reported the rank injustice, robbery and murder that they have been forced to witness day by day. Their duty to the world and to civilization compelled them to do this. Any ruler who wishes to govern by robbery and crime, and who openly disregards the ordinary laws of human rights, is embarrassed by the presence of missionaries for whose expulsion from the country he can find no proper excuse, and whom he dares not kill. It requires no demonstration to show why Russia has not wished missionaries among her people, and why, even now, the missionary is practically excluded from that country. An educated and thinking peasantry would not be helpful to the Russian methods of administration.

The story of the progress of missions reveals many cases where early official hostility has been changed into most hearty commendation. The original statement that the natives of some of the most uncivilized countries were incapable of education, has been overthrown by the exhibition in those countries of educated natives. The assumption that they were morally corrupt beyond reform, has been proved to be false by multitudes of morally upright Christians among them who cheerfully endured persecution and even death if need be for their faith. The belief that they were industrially low and incapable of advancement, has been met by the exhibit of well-trained, thrifty, artisans, merchants, and business men who demonstrated their ability to earn their way with industry and skill. Among many wild tribes and rude races of men, miracles have been wrought by missionary effort, and those who have observed have been compelled to admire, even if for personal reasons they have withheld open approval.

The traveler and brief sojourner in any country sees only the present conditions, and is not able to judge accurately of the progress that has been made, or of the true value of the work of the missionaries. There is no one better able to pass judgment than the local ruler or governor, who may be prejudiced against the missionary as a Christian worker, and may even question the wisdom of educating the natives.

It must be remembered that in some of the non-Christian countries missionaries have been carrying on work for one, two or even three generations. In many of these countries they inaugurated the first attempt at modern education, and erected the first modern hospital the people had ever seen. While some of the native or foreign rulers have no sympathy with Christianity, there are few indeed who do not recognize the great value of the influence of the institutions the missionaries have planted. Some of the highest praise accorded missionary work has come from men who openly declared themselves to be out of sympathy with Christianity. In all countries missionaries are more than mere religious instructors; they are teachers of the true way of living and thinking, and arouse in the people whom they reach ambitions for that which is higher and better than the old life.

ILLUSTRATIVE QUOTATIONS

1. *The Earl of Northbrook:* " In the roll of men who have been active supporters of Christianity, of missions, will be found the most distinguished administrators and the best soldiers that have been in India—administrators and soldiers who are the pride of this country. Let us look for a moment at the names of these men. We have in the first place, and the oldest of all, Sir John Shore, afterwards Lord Teignmouth, one of the most able civil servants of his time. We have Robert Bird, a name probably known to very few here now, but known in India as that of one of the ablest administrators of the country. We have seen James Thomason, the son of a chaplain, Lieutenant-Governor of the Northwestern Provinces, under whom these distinguished men who were the safeguard of India in the time of the Mutiny received their training. We have John Lawrence, Henry Lawrence, Robert Montgomery, Donald McLeod, who was called one of the angels of India. I can confirm this by the fact that a small deputation of natives from the Punjab once came to see me, who worshipped the photograph of Donald McLeod. We have Reynell Taylor, who started the Church Missionary Mission on the other side of the Indus. We have Robert Cust, who is still among us, and Herbert Edwardes. But I must add those with whom I myself have worked in India. We have William Nuir and Henry Norman, who, when a very young man, was one of the men who started the first mission at Peshawar. We have Richard Temple, whom I see here to-day. We

have Charles Aitchison, Rivers Thompson, and Henry Ramsay."

2. *The Maharajah of Travancore, a native ruler:* "Long before the State itself undertook the humanizing task of educating the subject population, the Christian missionaries had raised the beacon of knowledge in this land. One cannot be sufficiently thankful for the introduction of this civilizing element, and its happily steady development. Your labors have been increasing, year after year, the number of a loyal, law-abiding, and civilized population—the very foundation of good government."

3. *Sir C. U. Aitchison, Lieutenant-Governor of the Punjab:* "The changes that are to-day being wrought out by Christian missionaries in India are simply marvelous. Teaching wherever they go the universal brotherhood of man, and animated by a faith which goes beyond the ties of family caste and relationship, Christian missionaries are slowly, but none the less surely, undermining the foundations of Hindu superstition, and bringing about a peaceful, religious, and moral and social revolution."

4. *Governor of Shansi, China:* "I, the Governor, find, then, having made myself acquainted with the facts, that the chief work of the Christian religion is in all places to exhort men to live virtuously. From the time of their entrance into China, Christian missionaries have given medicine gratuitously to the sick, and distributed money in times of famine. They expend large sums in charity, and diligently superintend its distribution. They regard other men as they do themselves, and make no difference between this country and that. Yet we Chinese, whether

people or scholars, constantly look askance on them as professing a foreign religion, and have treated them not with generous kindness but with injustice and contempt, for which we ought to feel ashamed. Contrasting the way in which we have been treated by the missionaries with our treatment of them, how can anyone who has the least regard for right and reason not feel ashamed of this behavior?"

5. *Sir William Mackworth Young, K. C. S. I., Lieutenant-Governor of the Punjab, India:* "As a business man speaking to business men, I am prepared to say that the work which has been done by missionary agency in India exceeds in importance all that has been done (and much has been done) by the British Government in India since its commencement.

"Let me take the province which I know best. I ask myself what has been the most potent influence which has been working among the people since annexation—fifty-four years ago—and to that question I feel there is but one answer: Christianity, as set forth in the lives and teachings of Christian missionaries.

"If the natives of India have any practical knowledge of what is meant by Christian charity, if they know anything of high, disinterested motives and self-sacrifice, it is mainly from the missionaries that they learn it. The strength of our position in India depends more largely on the good will of the people than upon the strength and number of our garrison, and for that good will we are largely indebted to the kindly, self-sacrificing efforts of the Christian missionary in his dealing with the people."

6. *Sir Augustus Rivers-Thompson, Lieutenant-Governor of Bengal:* "In my judgment Christian mission-

aries have done more real and lasting good to the people of India than all other agencies combined. They have been the salt of the country, and the true saviors of the empire."

7. *Prince Damrong, Minister of the Interior for Siam, to the Hon. Hamilton King, United States Minister to Siam:* "I want to say to you that we have great respect for your American missionaries in our country, and appreciate very highly the work they are doing for our people. I want this to be understood by everyone, and if you are in a position to let it be known to your countrymen, I wish you would say this for me. The work of your people is excellent."

8. *Report of the South African Native Affairs Commission 1903-1905, Sir Godfrey Lagden, Chairman:* "For the moral improvement of the natives there is available no influence equal to that of religious belief.

"The Commission is of the opinion that hope for the elevation of the native races must depend mainly on their acceptance of Christian faith and morals.

"The weight of evidence is in favor of the improved morality of the Christian section of the population, and to the effect that there appears to be in the native mind no inherent incapacity to apprehend the truths of Christian teaching or to adopt Christian morals as a standard. It does not seem practicable to propose any measure of material support or aid to the purely spiritual side of missionary enterprise, but the commission recommends full recognition of the utility of the work of the churches which have undertaken the duty of evangelizing the heathen.

9. *Marquis Ito, Prime Minister of Japan:* "Japan's progress and development are largely due to the influence of missionaries exerted in right directions when Japan was first studying the outer world."

10. *Lord Napier, Governor of Madras, India:* "My travels in this Presidency are now drawing to a close, but when I shall revert to them in the midst of other engagements and other scenes, memory will offer no more attractive pictures than those which will reproduce the features of missionary life. In Ganjore, in Masulipatam, in North Arcot, in Travancore, in Tinnevelli, in Tanjore, I have broken the missionary's bread, I have been present at his ministrations, I have witnessed his teachings, I have seen the beauty of his life. In the matter of education, the co-operation of the religious societies is, of course, inestimable to the Government and its people. Missionary agency is, in my judgment, the only agency that can at present bring the benefits of teaching home to the humblest orders of the population.

"The benefits of missionary enterprise are felt in three directions, in converting, civilizing, and teaching the Indian people. It is not easy to overrate the value in this vast empire of a class of Englishmen of pious lives and disinterested labors, living and moving in the most forsaken places, walking between the government and the people, with devotion to both—friends of right, adversaries of wrong, impartial spectators of good and evil."

11. *Sir John Woodburn, Lieutenant-Governor of Bengal:* "Speaking of Chota Nagpur, I was thinking of the surprise that arrived there even to so old an Indian as myself. We are accustomed to think of the savage tribes in these hills as almost irreclaimable from the naked

barbarism of their nomad life. What did I find? In the schools of the missionaries there were scores of Kol boys rapidly attaining university standards in education. It was to me a revelation that the savage intellect, which we are all apt to regard as dwarft and dull, and inapt, is as acute and quick to acquire as that of the son of generations of culture. It seems incredible, but it is a fact, that the Kol lads are walking straight into the lists of competition on equal terms with the high-bred youth of Bengal. This is a circumstance so strange, so striking, so full of significance for the future, that I could not refrain from telling you of this last surprise of this wonderful land we live in."

12. *General Sir Charles Warren, Governor of Natal:* " For the preservation of peace between the colonists and natives, one missionary is worth a battalion of soldiers."

13. *Mr. Tripp, United States Commissioner to the Samoan Islands in* 1899: " These people [the Samoans] are far from being savages. They are splendid specimens of physical manhood, and are well informed about matters of general information. They are nearly all Christians, and are very devout in their attachment to their church and religion. Thanks to the missionaries the great bulk of the natives and nearly all the chiefs can read and write and are adopting the habits of civilization with great alacrity."

14. *Count Okuma, Prime Minister and leading states-man in Japan:* " It is a question whether as a people we have not lost moral fiber as a result of the many new influences to which we have been subjected. Development has been intellectual and not moral. The efforts which

Christians are making to supply to the country a high standard of conduct are welcomed by all right-thinking people. As you read your Bible you may think it is antiquated, out of date. The words it contains may so appear, but the noble life which it holds up to admiration is something that will never be out of date, however much the world may progress. Live and preach this life and you will supply to the nation just what it needs at the present juncture."

15. *King Lewanika of the Barotsis:* "Where are the white men that before this have ever taken the pains to construct buildings like this, not for their own exclusive use, but for us? Do you not see, then, that there is something in the breasts of these men, the missionaries? What do they make by fatiguing themselves so for us? Tell me! And you, Barotsis, who despise their instructions and refuse to send your children to their school, are you then so wise and intelligent? Perish our customs and our superstitions! They hold us enchained in darkness and conduct us to ruin. I see it!"

16. *Sir W. MacGregor, Governor of British New Guinea:* "It can never be overlooked that the pioneers in civilizing this place were the members of the London Missionary Society. The work of the Society in this country I probably value higher than does any other person, but that is only because I know it better. Although not the first mission in this colony, it was the first that could obtain a permanent footing and make its influence felt. What your mission has already effected here in the work of humanity can never be forgotten or ignored in the history of the colony, and the great names of Chalmers and Lawes will long continue to be incen-

tives to younger men to keep the mission up to its former and present high standard of usefulness, while steadily enlarging its field. Will you kindly convey to the ministers and teachers of the mission my sincere and cordial thanks for their loyal co-operation, and assure them of my lasting sympathy with them in their unselfish and generous task in British New Guinea?"

17. *A Japanese commanding officer (after the expedition to relieve Peking):* "I am not a believer myself, but I have noted among the troops the good conduct of those who are Christians, the quiet, fearless way in which they go bravely into battle, and the orderly, collected way in which they bear themselves afterwards, free from excitement prejudicial to discipline. I think it would be a good thing for the army if all became Christians."

18. *Sir Richard Temple, Lieutenant-Governor of Bengal:* "I have governed one hundred and five millions of the inhabitants of India, and I have been concerned with eighty-five millions more in my official capacity. I have thus had acquaintance with or have been authentically informed regarding nearly all the missionaries of the societies laboring in India within the last thirty years. And what is my testimony regarding these men? They are most efficient."

19. *Sir W. Hunter, author of the "Imperial Gazette" of India:* "The careless onlooker may have no particular convictions on the subject, and flippant persons may ridicule religious effort in India as elsewhere. But I think that few Indian administrators have passed through high office and had to deal with ultimate problems of British government in that country without feeling the value of

the work done by the missionaries. Such men gradually realize, as I have realized, that the missionaries do really represent the spiritual side of the new civilization, and of the new life which we are introducing into India."

20. *The Marquis of Salisbury:* " The Government had learned to know the use of missionaries in East Africa. In all departments of life the missionary there was essential to progress."

21. *Admiral Wilkes:* "The moral reformation of the Pacific Islanders is pre-eminently due to the exertions of the London Missionary Society."

22. *Sir Muncherjee Bharnajgree, a Parsee member of Parliament:* " American missionaries are doing more for the industrial development of the Indian Empire than the Government itself."

23. *Lord Northcote, Governor of the Bombay Presidency, in a letter to President Roosevelt:* "In Ahmednagar I have seen for myself what practical results have been accomplished, and during the famine we owed much to the practical schemes of benevolence of the American missionaries."

24. *Chulalongkorn, King of Siam:* "American missionaries have done more to advance the welfare of my country and people than any other foreign influence."

25. *Baron Maejima, Cabinet officer in Japan:* "I firmly believe we must have religion as the basis of our national and personal welfare. No matter how large an army or navy we may have, unless we have righteous-

ness at the foundation of our national existence we shall fall short of the highest success. I do not hesitate to say that we must rely upon religion for our highest welfare. And when I look about me to see what religion we may best rely upon, I am convinced that the religion of Christ is the one most full of strength and promise for the nation."

26. *Sir Peregrine Maitland, Governor of Cape Colony:* "I have relied more upon the labors of the missionaries for the peaceful government of the natives than upon the presence of British troops."

27. *King of Korea:* "There are many, many Americans in Korea. We are glad they are here. Thank the American people, and we shall be glad to receive more teachers."

28. *Lieutenant-Governor of New Guinea:* "I would venture to say that the Government owes everything to missions. I wish I could make our people fully realize what the missions mean to the Administration. It would have to be doubled, perhaps quadrupled in strength, if it were not for the little whitewashed houses along the coast where the missionaries live. Every penny contributed to this mission is a help to the Queen's Government! Every penny spent by the missionaries saves pounds to the Administration, for the missions bring peace, law, and order. Missionaries help the Government, and the Government is proud to reciprocate the aid."

29. *Report of the Secretary of State and Council of India:* "The whole subject of missionary enterprise in India has such an important bearing on the intellectual

advancement of the people that any notice of Indian education would be incomplete without giving some details respecting the work of missionaries."

30. *Viceroy Tuan Fong of China; Special Commissioner to the United States:* "We take pleasure in bearing testimony to the part taken by American missionaries in promoting the progress of the Chinese people. They have borne the light of Western civilization into every nook and corner of the empire. The awakening of China which now seems to be at hand, may be traced in no small measure to the hands of the missionaries. For this service you will find China not ungrateful."

31. *The Hon. Chester Holcombe, diplomat and author:* "In many years of intimate official and friendly inter-course with all classes of Chinese in every part of the Empire, the writer has never heard even one complaint of or objection to the presence of American missionaries in China, or the character of their work. He has heard himself, and all other foreigners of every nationality and calling, cursed in most violent terms for having fastened the opium horror upon the Chinese race, and the sug-gestion made, in a paroxysm of anger and hate by some human wreck wrought by the drug, that foreigners ' would do well to take away that awful curse before they had the impudence to talk to the Chinese about their Jesus.' But, aside from crazed and mistaken denunciation, no Chinaman within his hearing has had anything but pleas-ant words to speak regarding the missionary enterprise, as conducted by Americans, in his land."

VIII

THE CHARACTER AND ABILITY OF THE MISSIONARY

ONE well may hesitate to say anything upon a subject so personal, and one which is in the judgment of those who know best, unnecessary to discuss. Is not the missionaries' well-known record sufficient to demonstrate to the world their superior ability and their high and noble character? All who are informed in regard to their work will at once say "yes." To these we might as well attempt to prove that the sun gives us light and heat as to prove that foreign missionaries are men and women of exalted integrity and unusual ability. For such this chapter is not written. There are some, and they are not a small number, who seem to delight to refer to the missionary in patronizing terms or to speak of him apologetically. To such these few words are directed.

It should be stated at the outset that no true friend of the missionaries will place them upon pedestals, or regard them in any other light than as men and women of like passions with ourselves. They have not all the same capacities, and in temperament and characteristics they differ widely from one another. You cannot characterize missionaries by any single term, any more than you can doctors or lawyers. Some of them have made failures and have been compelled to withdraw from the work, some have had indifferent success, while others, and these constitute the large majority, have proved themselves admirably fitted for the work. These are the ones who, under God, have made foreign missions a power in the world.

There is no doubt that some mission organizations yet require few qualifications for missionary appointment beyond a devout spirit and a burning desire to enter the service. But gradually it is becoming apparent to all, that admirable and necessary as are the above qualifications, they are not sufficient in themselves to make a man or a woman a successful missionary in any country in the world.

The long established and largest mission boards put all their candidates through a rigid examination and subject them to wide investigation before accepting them as missionaries. Many applicants are declined because, in some one or more important features, they fail to come up to the required standard. No one knows better than do the officers of the mission boards how inadequate and fallible are all those tests, yet they constitute at present the best way known for the selection of missionaries. The purpose of all boards is to secure and appoint only those who seem to be called of the Lord for this service, and who give every promise of devoting a long life to the successful prosecution of the work of propagating Christianity.

Experience has seemed to demonstrate that all things else being equal, the fully and broadly-educated man or woman is likely to be the most successful. On the whole, a foreign missionary requires a better education than the pastor at home. The Congregational churches of America have always demanded an educated ministry. No denomination in the world boasts so many higher educational institutions. And yet, the percentage of university trained men now under appointment by the American Board is about 95 of the whole number of commissioned men, while the percentage of such men in the Congregational ministry in the United States is reported to be only about 65. Since there are now so many native Christian workers in many mission fields who bear university degrees and so much of the work of missions has to do with the training of native Christian leaders, the importance of the most complete educational equipment will not diminish.

The percentage of university trained men under the other leading boards may not be as great as the above, but the educational qualifications demanded in the missionary are not less than those demanded by the home churches in their ministry. There is no profession outside the University professorships where the percentage of university-trained men is higher than it is among the foreign missionaries of the leading mission boards. It should be added that most of these men have had in addition from three to five years of technical training in a theological or medical school and some in both.

As soon as the missionary reaches his field, he is compelled to master a foreign language and make it his own. Some of those languages, like the Japanese, the Chinese, the Tamil, and Marathi of India, and the

Arabic, are the most difficult languages spoken by men. Captain Brinkley, a profound Japanese scholar, and editor of the *Japan Mail,* once told the writer that in his judgment one could master, so as to use fluently, all of the languages of Europe, including Russian, as easily as he can learn to use with accuracy and ease the language of Japan. While this may be an overstatement, it makes clear the fact that the Japanese missionary must put to the severest test an already well-trained mind before he can even begin to do missionary work in the vernacular which most missionaries are required to learn.

There is no doubt that the mental effort and persistent application demanded, in many mission countries, to fit the missionary even to begin his work, if expended in a German or American university, would secure for the man the degrees of Master of Arts or Doctor of Philosophy, or both. By the time the missionary begins his work in the vernacular, he has experienced a course of mental discipline equalled by that demanded in few other professions. This ought to be sufficient to insure mental balance and guarantee that he is no weakling.

Apart from their mental equipment most missionaries pass through a spiritual experience which exerts a strong influence upon their characters. They deliberately choose to follow a career that promises them, in financial returns, a mere support so long as they serve, with little assurance of a pension when disabled, and without opportunity to earn money independently. The so-called salaries paid missionaries by different boards differ slightly, but the general rule is that they shall not exceed the cost of a fair living at the place where the missionaries are located. It is not an easy matter for a strong, vigorous man or woman to decide to enter upon a life-work which promises, from year to year in financial returns, practically nothing beyond a simple living.

To this is added the decision to spend that life of chosen poverty in a foreign land, in most cases, amid unfavorable surroundings, far away from personal friends, among people who misunderstand his motives and misinterpret his acts. In his life the missionary faces with the people the uncertainties of pestilence, and he always is amid the unsanitary conditions of uncivilized lands. Whatever may be said, viewed from a merely physical standpoint, the life of the missionary is full of personal sacrifice from beginning to end. This itself ought to develop strength of character and a charm that is hard to attain unto in lands where no such sacrifice is called for. The demands made upon him in the work cannot fail to develop him.

Apart from the purely evangelistic part of their labors, the missionaries in most countries have organized, developed and put into operation, a system of education extending from the kindergarten and primary schools of the villages, up through all grades to the college and theological seminary. Many of these mission colleges stand to-day at the very head and center of the entire educational system of those countries. Some of these institutions have become independent and have a reputation that is world wide.

CHARACTER AND ABILITY

The entire modern educational system of the Turkish Empire was introduced into the country and developed by missionaries. The same is practically true of China, India, Ceylon, Africa, and, in fact, almost every mission country in the world. The superior ability of many of these missionary educators has been frequently recognized by various governments and local officials. The results accomplished, taken together with the almost insuperable obstacles that had to be overcome, are in themselves the highest possible tribute to the character and ability of the men and women who wrested victory out of conditions that gave no promise when the work began.

In many of these countries the missionaries not only had to reduce the spoken language to writing, but thereafter were compelled to create in that language an educational and a religious literature. This literature covered the widest scope of schoolbooks from the simple primer to the grammar and dictionary, including books on the sciences and philosophical works. It also included a periodical and permanent religious literature, beginning with the translation of the Bible and embracing treatises on ethics and religion. Missionary literature covers the widest possible range and has required for its production exact knowledge, and most careful, painstaking research.

In addition to this phase of work, missionaries have been most active in their study of the countries in which they were located. Such a knowledge of the country and people is absolutely essential to the best success of the work. Probably no other single class of people have added so much to the world's positive knowledge of geography and ethnology as have missionaries. They have explored, and mapped, and reported, with precision and accuracy, and missionary reports in the archives of the older missionary societies, and the missionary articles in the files of scientific journals are full of information that could have been obtained from no other source. The value of these contributions is fully recognized by learned societies.

Since the missionary is by training a student, and as his labors bring him constantly into relations with the religious beliefs and practices of the people, he has been a master student of religions and has furnished the world the most extended data for the study of religions. The science of comparative religion owes more to the missionaries than to any other class of people.

The science of medicine has gained not a little from the experiences of medical missionaries in the uncivilized countries of the world, and among the physicians who have been sent out by the various mission boards have been some of the most renowned and influential physicians and surgeons known to the profession. It was inevitable that this should be the case with men of the widest general and professional training thrown into the midst of conditions which demanded the exercise of every resource.

Without prolonging these lists, to which there can be found no end, we can easily understand that the right kind of a missionary has every incentive to develop both mentally and spiritually, and the conditions are usually such that he must develop in a multitude of directions.

We at home often are led to misjudge the missionary because we do not see him at advantage. By long residence abroad he has got out of touch with American ways and life. He often shrinks from the demands of society and from its formalities, and rebels against its apparent insincerities. Long use of some vernacular or vernaculars may have made him halt in the use of the English language. He feels out of place in this country, and is eager to get back to his work and people. Some have interpreted these things as indications of mental weakness, and have concluded that missionaries are neither educated nor refined people If one wishes to see the missionaries at their best and in their true light, he must go with them about their fields and see them surrounded by their co-laborers and in the midst of their work. He will there see that they are masters of their positions, genuine organizers, and inspired leaders of men.

The missionary takes up his abode in a foreign country for life. There he devotes himself with his years of careful training to the work of organizing a permanent and self-propagating, industrious Christian society, from which shall grow Christian institutions of all grades and kinds. He creates this society from crude material, and out of it produces results that, from our human standpoint, seem miraculous. He shows himself to be a friend of the common people as well as a loyal guest of the local government. He turns disorder into victory, and little by little produces ripe fruits of the Kingdom of God. Viewed from every standpoint the missionary of character and ability stands easily first among leaders of men and benefactors of the world.

ILLUSTRATIVE QUOTATIONS

1. *William McKinley, President of the United States:* " The missionary, of whatever church or ecclesiastical body, carrying the torch of truth and enlightenment, deserves the gratitude, the support, and the homage of mankind. The noble, self-effacing, willing ministers of peace and good will should be classed with the world's heroes."

2. *Mr. Walter C. Hillier, of the British Consular Service:* " Lives which bear every mark of transparent simplicity and truthfulness, that will stand the test of the severest scrutiny, must, in the end, have their due effect. It seems presumptuous to offer a tribute of praise to men [missionaries] whose literal interpretation of the calls of duty have placed them almost beyond the reach of popular commendation, but perhaps I may be allowed to say that anyone who has seen the lives that these men are leading cannot fail to feel proud of being able to claim them as countrymen of his own."

3. *Mr. Joseph Thomson, African traveler:* " No one is a more sincere admirer of the missionary than I; no one knows better the noble lives of many, the singleness of purpose with which they pursue the course they think the only true one. They seem to me the best and truest heroes which this nineteenth century has produced. . .

150

" In the heart of the Dark Continent I have been received as a brother, I have been relieved when I was destitute, I have been nursed when I was half dead, and time after time I have been sent on my weary way, rejoicing that there is such a profession of men as the Christian missionary."

4. *Sir Philip Currie, British Ambassador to Constantinople,* 1896: " The one bright spot in the darkness that has covered Asiatic Turkey has been the heroism and common sense of the American missionaries."

5. *An English Ambassador at Constantinople,* when asked by the Duke of Westminster to name someone to distribute the relief funds raised in England for the suffering Armenians, replied, " Send no one; employ the American missionaries. No one knows the people or their wants so well, and none are so capable."

6. *Rev. Endicott Peabody, head master of the Groton school in Massachusetts:* " I have much to do with boys, and I would rather have one of my boys become a foreign missionary than President. The work of missionaries is the grandest in the whole world, and the missionaries are the heroes of modern times."

7. *An officer who made a tour of observation in Eastern Turkey a few years ago at the expense of the Sultan:* " The most zealous advocate of American civilization could not have done half as much for his country abroad as the missionary has done. What Dr. Hamlin is silently doing with his Robert College and the American missionary with his theological seminary and schoolbooks, all European diplomats united cannot overbalance."

8. *Professor Louis Agassiz:* "Few are aware how much we owe them [the missionaries] both for their intelligent observation of facts and for their collecting of specimens. We must look to them not a little for aid in our efforts to advance future science."

9. *Mrs. Isabella Bird Bishop, traveler and author:* "I am a traveler solely, and it is as a traveler that I desire to bear my testimony to the godly and self-denying lives, the zeal, and the devotion of nearly all the missionaries of all the churches that I have everywhere seen. This testimony from a traveler unconnected with missions may be, I trust, of some value, and I am prepared to give it everywhere."

10. *Sir Henry M. Stanley, explorer:* "What mission in Africa can show such splendid results as this of Uganda? If we regard the number of converts instructed in the Protestant faith, the cruelties inflicted on them and their pastors, the magnificent endurance exhibited during their severe trials, the vast patience, and the unflinching courage and meekness with which they have borne them during the last thirteen years, we shall have good cause to hold the missionaries in Uganda as among the brightest examples of Christian teachers ever sent from England to benighted regions."

11. *Sir Robert Hart:* "As for the missionary class, their devotion, zeal, and good works are recognized by all."

12. *Kanwar Sir Harnam Singh:* "I consider that among the manifold blessings of British rule in India, Christian missions occupy the most prominent place.

Friends and foes, Christians and non-Christians, have from time to time borne testimony to the noble work done by missionaries in India. They have been the pioneers in education and culture, and have been the champions of free thought and enlightened action. They have afforded sympathy to the people in their joy and sorrow, and have stood between them and their rulers in times of trouble and need. The people in all parts of the country keenly appreciate the self-sacrificing zeal with which they pursue the divine work they have undertaken: and who has not been touched by all that the missionaries have done for the people of India during the last famine, *i. e.,* even to the laying down of their lives? Suffice it then to say that the people of India owe a deep debt of gratitude to missions and missionaries."

13. *Horace N. Allen, U. S. Minister to Korea, former Consul to China:* "To those who insinuate that missionaries go abroad to raise themselves in the social scale, or for the sake of the loaves and fishes, I reply, knowing the conditions of missionary work, that such would very soon come home disgusted and disappointed men. To those who talk of the inferiority of missionaries in China, I answer, study their record. I find a proportion of men of such ability that the accusation of inferiority is simply ludicrous. . . . Think of some of these when you next hear of the intellectual and social inferiority of the missionaries in China."

14. *Archdeacon Farrar:* "To sneer at missionaries—a thing so cheap and so easy to do—has always been the fashion of libertines and cynics and worldlings. So far from having failed, there is no work of God which has received so absolute, so unprecedented a blessing. To

talk of missionaries as a failure is to talk at once like an ignorant and like a faithless man.

"Is it nothing that through the labors of the missionaries in the translation of the Bible the German philologist in his study may have before him the grammar and vocabulary of two hundred and fifty languages? Who created the science of anthropology? The missionaries. Who rendered possible the deeply important science of comparative religions? The missionaries. Who discovered the great chain of lakes in Central Africa, on which will turn its future destiny? The missionaries. Who have been the chief explorers of Oceanica and America and Asia? The missionaries. Who discovered the famous Nestorian monument in Singan Fu? A Church missionary. Who discovered the Hittite inscriptions? A Presbyterian missionary."

15. *Meredith Townsend:* "The missionaries in India lead excellent and hard-working lives, are implicitly trusted by the whole community, European and native. Many of them become men of singular learning, many more show themselves administrators of high merit, and all display on occasion that reserve of energy and devotion which more than any other thing marks that the heart of the service is sound."

16. *Babu Dakinaranjan Mukerji, India:* "However we may differ with the Christian missionaries in religion, I speak the minds of our society and generally of those of the people, when I say that as regards their learning, purity of morals, and disinterestedness of intention to promote our weal, no doubt is entertained throughout the land: nay, they are held by us in the highest esteem. European history does not bear on its record the mention

of a class of men who suffered so many sacrifices in the cause of humanity and education as the Christian missionaries in India."

17. *Rev. John Watson (Ian Maclaren):* "We second-rate fellows here at home are the militia: a very respectable lot of hard-working men, but just militia! They are the fighting-line—theirs are the medals with the bars—they are our Victoria Cross men!"

18. *Mr. A. J. Fraser-Blair, Editor of "The English-man":* "The missionaries have, practically unaided, created modern India. I am now, of course, regarding their work from a purely political and educational point of view, leaving its religious aspect to be dealt with by those better qualified to review it than myself. If we carefully consider the careers of Warren Hastings and Alexander Duff, and mark their effect upon history, which, weighing everything, shall we say did more for India, the English adventurer or the Scottish missionary? And, looking to Warren Hastings' successors, may it not be truthfully asserted that the glittering procession of titled persons who have held high office in India during a century and a half have left it very much as they found it, while every missionary teacher throughout the same period has been the center of influences which are now transforming the whole Eastern world?"

19. *Lord Curzon, Viceroy of India, quoted by William E. Curtis:* "I have seen cases where the entire organization of a vast area and the lives of thousands of beings rested upon the shoulders of a single individual, laboring on in silence, and in solitude, while his bodily strength was fast ebbing away. I have known of natives who, in-

spired by his example, have thrown themselves with equal
ardor into the struggle, and have unmurmuringly laid
down their lives for their countrymen. Particularly must
I mention the noble efforts of missionary agencies of
various Christian denominations. If there ever was an
occasion in which it was open to vindicate the highest
standards of their beneficent calling it was here, and
strenuously and faithfully have they performed the task."

20. *John W. Foster, Secretary of State, diplomat, in
"American Diplomacy in the Orient," after speaking of
individual cases where different missionaries had rendered
signal services, adds:* " These instances are cited to show
what an important part the missionaries have borne in
the international relations of the Pacific. The instances
might be multiplied, and a detailed examination of these
relations will disclose that up to the middle of the last
century the Christian missionaries were an absolute necessity to diplomatic intercourse."

21. *Sir Harry H. Johnston, English traveler and
scholar:* " Indirectly and most unintentionally, missionary enterprise has widely increased the bounds of our
knowledge, and has sometimes been the means of con-
ferring benefits on science, the value and extent of which
itself was careless to appreciate and compute. Huge is
the debt which philologists owe to the labors of missionaries in Africa.

" By evangelists of our nationality nearly two hundred
African languages and dialects have been illustrated by
grammars, dictionaries, vocabularies, and translations of
the Bible. Many of these tongues were on the point of
extinction, and have since become extinct, and we owe
our knowledge of them solely to the missionaries' inter-

vention. Zoology, botany, and anthropology, and most of the other branches of scientific investigation have been enriched by the researches of missionaries, who have enjoyed opportunities of collecting in new districts."

22. *Philip Knobel, Minister from Holland to China:* "Christian missionaries are men of sterling character, able and high-principled. Wherever you find the missionary you find in his wake prosperity. He it is who has taught the ignorant native a higher art of agriculture, an improved industry, as well as a better religion."

23. *Sir Richard Temple, Lieutenant-Governor of Bengal, Governor of Bombay, and Finance Minister of India:* "Missionaries have contributed greatly to the culture of the vernacular languages, and many of them as scholars, historians, sociologists, or lexicographers have held a high place in Oriental literature, and have written books of lasting fame and utility."

24. *Sir William Mackworth Young, K. C. S. I., Lieutenant-Governor of the Punjab, India:* "The schools and colleges of the Christian missionaries are to be found in most of the large centers throughout India. The teaching which is given in them leaves nothing to be desired and the people themselves are well content to send their children to the mission schools. In fact, they rather prefer them, partly because the standard of teaching is higher and the staff of supervisors superior, but also because there is moral and religious training given in their schools and the native of India knows perfectly well how to appreciate that. The mission schools have turned out some of our most valuable officers. They have set a standard which has been of incalculable value to

the Department of Education generally. For this work the missionaries are entitled to the deep gratitude of the administration."

25. *The Rev. Professor John P. Peters, Ph. D., D. D., Sc. D., explorer and author:* " Seventeen years ago I made my first visit to Constantinople. I confess that when I first came in contact with the missionaries there it was with a certain prejudice. I looked on them with considerable distrust, as men proselyting from the ancient Christian churches of the country in the interests of a sect. I had not been long among them when I came to feel that they and I were brothers in every regard, and that anything I could do to further their work I would do with all my heart and soul. I found that because of them and their work the name of America was held in honor throughout Turkey, even beyond those regions where the work of the American missionaries was known. The reason was plain. The people from America whom the natives met and with whom exclusively they associated the name and idea of America were most highly educated, cultured, unselfish, and full of spirituality. Consequently the great mass of the people of the country knew Americans from their best side only. I found that, when I supposed I was where no American had ever gone, the honorable name and reputation of America had preceded me, thanks to the grand work done by the American missionaries.

26. *The Hon. Chester Holcombe, diplomat and author:* " From the inception of what may be termed modern missionary enterprise in China, the missionaries have gone beyond this narrow limit of favor, gone beyond the treaty ports, until now they can be found in every province and

in nearly every large city. Even in many mud-walled villages and rural hamlets missionary families are now to be found quietly and permanently established in homes, in close touch and intimate association with the native residents. This special favor, unobtainable by any other alien class in the Empire, has assuredly not been won either through any exercise of governmental force or diplomatic pressure. It has been slowly gained by the exercise of patience, tact, and discretion upon the part of the missionaries themselves, under the open eyes and with the tacit, though unspoken, consent of the Imperial authorities. In rare cases, missionaries have been driven out of interior points by local hostility; but in no instance has the Pekin government demanded their withdrawal, or our own government urged their right of residence there. This successful missionary expansion, as it may be called, speaks volumes for the wisdom and patient zeal of those who have accomplished it. It does more than this. It shows clearly a line of policy and procedure, which has now been consistently followed by the Imperial authorities for more than forty years, and which may here be stated. The Emperor will neither force nor forbid the residence and labors of missionaries at any points beyond the treaty ports. But recognizing and appreciating the self-denying and philanthropic character of missionary effort, he will gladly permit those engaged in it to establish themselves throughout the interior, wherever they may be able to do so with the consent and good will of the people of the locality. It is not known that this well-established line of policy has been formulated and officially communicated to any foreign power. But it has been verbally declared to the writer by members of the Cabinet and other high authorities of the Empire upon many occasions."

159

IX

THE MISSIONARY AND LUXURIOUS LIVING

IF it were possible to secure a general consensus of judgment from a large number of people as to how a missionary ought to live in order to exert the most profound and permanent influence over the people to whom he is sent, there would probably be practical unanimity in the conclusion that he ought not to live in what is called "luxury," even if such privileges were to be provided by the missionary society that supports him. There would also be a general feeling, upon the part of all, that if the missionary had abundant means of his own he ought not, in the interest of the work, to make display of his wealth and surround himself with luxuries which would largely remove him from the common people. A missionary is commonly regarded as one who has given up much that we all enjoy in this country, and has gone to a foreign, and often a dangerous, land, to devote his life to its elevation and Christianization. There are many who have formed in their minds a conception of the missionary living rudely, without any of the common comforts of life, enduring the severest hardships and perils amid most forbidding surroundings. This conception has become so thoroughly fixed in the minds of many good Christians in civilized countries, that it

160

is something of a shock to them to know that the missionary ordinarily lives in a comfortable house with a good roof over his head, and a comfortable bed to sleep upon at night, and that he has daily sufficient food for the proper nourishment of his body. This is quite contrary to the conception of those who think of the missionary as emaciated, worn, pale, and diseased. Some have cherished this conception to such an extent that for them to know that a missionary has any of the ordinary comforts and necessaries of life is to lead them to lose faith in the class, and to assume that the missionary is not devoted to his work and is not doing that for which he was sent. Such persons would regard the missionary always as an ascetic, mortifying his body, enduring unnecessary hardships, in order that in some mystical way he might bring the people to whom he goes to a recognition of Jesus Christ as Redeemer and Lord. They can never give their reasons why the one who goes abroad to preach the Gospel of Jesus Christ should thus endure hardships not demanded by the work he is sent to do, and, as I hope to show later, not helpful to the progress of that work, but rather a hindrance to it.

As has already been shown, missionary candidates reach a position where they can be sent to the work only after many years of preparation, and even then, those who are sent are selected from a still larger number of those who would like to go, but who, for various reasons, are not sufficiently equipped in body, mind, or temperament for the work. When, out of the large number of applicants, a few are chosen and set apart for this special work, it is with the understanding that they enter upon this work for life. It is expected that as they go out at the beginning of their career, this life will be from twenty to fifty or sixty years, and that it will be devoted entirely to the missionary work to which they have been appointed. There are at present missionaries in connection with the oldest missionary boards who have been in the field from forty-five to fifty-five or sixty years, devoting themselves during all these years to the work to which they were sent. Not long since Dr. Elias Riggs, a missionary of the American Board, passed away in Constantinople after sixty-nine years of persistent service under that board for the people of Turkey. This is what is meant by a life-service in the mission field.

For a missionary to become generally useful in the missionary field, and to bear his part of the work, requires from three to six years of preparation. The expense, therefore, of getting a missionary upon the field, apart from the original expense of mental equipment in the schools, is not inconsiderable. This means a housekeeping outfit of from five to six hundred dollars for his family, and perhaps as much more to pay the traveling expenses to the mission; moreover, he must remain in a measure unproductive from three to six years in the field while he is learning the language or languages of the mission, and getting himself ready for the fullest and largest service. If, during this period, the missionary's health breaks down, and he is compelled to give up the work and return home, all of the money, or most of the money that has been spent on his outfit, traveling expenses, and support, while studying the language and learning the work, is practically thrown away.

This makes it very clear why it is necessary that in selecting missionaries the greatest care should be taken, and also why the missionary himself should guard his health and strength, so that when he is ready for the service for which he has been appointed, he can bring to that service the best physical and mental strength at his command. Short lives, ordinarily, in the mission field are of little direct value to the work. There are marked exceptions to this where, through some special emergency or hardship a missionary has been called early in his career to lay down his life. Such was the case with Harriet Newell, who never reached the field to which she was sent, nor saw the people for whom she had given her life. And yet by her early death she has exerted a boundless influence upon the women who have followed her in their thoughts and interests, and has turned many to the missionary work. The same may be well said of Horace Pitkin, who after only two or three years in the mission field, was called to lay down his life as he was attempting to defend the missionary women at Pao-ting-fu in the Boxer uprising of 1900. But these are exceptions to the general rule. In the ordinary course of events, the missionary who can give the longest life of service to the cause is the one who brings the strongest influence to bear upon the people among whom he lives, and who will produce the largest results by his life. It is the missionary's duty to invest his life in the way that will bring forth the largest and most permanent results, and experience has proved that, as a general thing, these results are not obtained by starving the body or misusing it by unnecessary hardships, or causing it to carry unnecessary burdens, and thus wearing it out early in its career.

New missionaries in going to the field are often surprised at the general comforts which surround the old missionaries in the field. Some, in preparing for the field, have left behind pictures for the walls and little knick-knacks that will make the home comfortable and pleasant and bring to mind the home-life which they have left behind. This is a mistake both from the missionary standpoint and from the standpoint of economy. The mind of the missionary can render the best service when it is the most at rest. These being facts which have become well established during the last century of modern missions, the old mission boards regard it as the wisest economy in the use of funds to select the best men and the best women available to the service to which they call them, and then, when they are once upon their field, to give them comfortable homes and to surround them with the ordinary comfortable necessaries of life, so that, physically and mentally, they shall be made to bear the least strain consistent with their missionary work, and so be able to devote their best physical, mental, and spiritual strength to the work of missions. Therefore, these mission boards for the most part provide for their missionaries comfortable houses, large and commodious, because of the mission work which centers in the home.

The home is often a gathering place for the people; often it is a meeting place where they assemble from day to day. Not infrequently a school is held in some part of the house or upon the veranda, or it may be within the grounds. The missionary's home is the center of his life and work, and from it go all sorts of beneficent influences to those who come in contact with it. This necessitates not only a comfortable place, but a commodious place in which he may live. In tropical countries the house must be larger than in cooler countries, so as to guard the missionary from the undue weakness and debilitation which come from extreme heat. At the same time it is required of him that he eat wholesome and abundant food, so that he may be in constant trim for whatever service may come to him. These are conditions that are not only permitted to missionaries, but are demanded of them by the boards that send them out and that furnish their support while they are engaged in the work. Any missionary who should neglect the ordinary rules of life, and fail to supply himself with the ordinary necessaries for keeping up his health and strength, should be called to an account by the missionary board in charge.

In India, where plague, cholera, and various tropical diseases rage through some seasons of the year, and are always present with the masses of the people, it is required of the missionary that his bungalow shall be reared somewhat apart from the houses of the people, so that, in times of plague, the missionary compounds may be kept as free from it as possible, thus enabling the missionary to make the compound a refuge, as it often is, for those who have escaped the plague. This is in a measure true of the houses of the missionaries in Turkey, although it is impossible often in Turkey to secure a house apart from the houses of the community, so that in Turkey more than in almost any other country, the missionaries often live in the closest relation with the people, and take their chances with them in times of plague or special distress. In Japan the houses of the missionaries appear larger and more luxurious than the houses of the people, so that to the casual observer or traveler passing through the country, the impression is often made that the missionary is living in luxury, compared with the manner of life of the Japanese themselves. That matter has been carefully looked into, and it has been found that the missionaries' quarters, although built in foreign style and appearing much larger than the more diminutive houses of the Japanese, cost less and are regarded by the Japanese as being greatly inferior in comfort to their own houses. The missionaries have attempted to live in Japanese houses, but found that because of their construction it is impossible for them to do so without suffering physically, and thus proving that it is poor enconomy to attempt it. The general experience has shown that for the missionaries in Japan it is better to build a house somewhat after the foreign style, although it is not considered by the Japanese as comfortable as their own houses, and the Japanese themselves do not believe that the missionaries live in luxury.

This preservation of the life of the missionary is necessary because of the fact that as the years go on his influence deepens and strengthens. One missionary remaining in the country and working for forty years exerts a more lasting influence and does a much more permanent and broader work than two men of equal strength and power could accomplish in twenty years. It is, therefore, of great importance that the missionaries remain for a long life, as in all Oriental countries the patriarch is highly honored and the missionary who has spent forty years among the people, during the remaining ten years, if he is permitted to labor so long, exerts a great deal more influence by his work and by his life than at any period in the previous forty years.

Some people are surprised that missionaries keep servants and do not do all their household work themselves. This is also a part of the question which has been discussed above. A deputation sent out by the American Board to India made a careful investigation of the servant question, and was surprised to find in one of the first cases investigated that the missionary had more than a dozen servants of one kind or another. The matter was gone through with most carefully, and it was learned that the cost of this whole body of servants—who, by the way, boarded themselves, as they did not like the food which the missionary ate— was less than the amount paid by one of the members of the deputation to a single maid-of-all-work at home. These servants lifted from the missionary's wife and the missionary the responsibility for the menial affairs connected with the home, and enabled the missionary and his wife to give their entire strength and time to direct missionary service. It was not necessary for the missionary to break off any conversation, or to withdraw from any public meeting, or to refuse to attend any meeting, or to respond to any calls of need which came in at any hour of the day, because he must do some menial service about the home, look after his horse or attend to some other matter connected with his domestic life. These details were looked after by those whom he employed at a trifling sum, and he was relieved, as was his wife, for the missionary work. In this way the whole time and strength of the missionary was available from morning until night, week in and week out, for direct, positive, aggressive missionary service. What is true in India is true in every country in the world. It would be the poorest kind of economy for any missionary board to allow its missionaries to spend any appreciable part of their time and strength in superfluous work about their home, or in any other place in the foreign field, provided a native could be employed to do that service. So many servants are not necessary in Turkey, or in Japan, or possibly in any other country, because the caste system does not prevail as in India. But one servant is a necessity in every missionary home in every mission land, in order to the wisest economy and the broadest use of the missionary's life.

There is another reason why the native servant is essential, and that is that in most Oriental countries the method of housekeeping is entirely different from that of the Occident. No Western woman going into the Orient could keep her health and do her cooking in the native kitchen with the native utensils. This itself is an art in which only the Orientals are proficient, and any Occidental woman attempting to learn that art and practice it, would necessarily break down in health and come home an invalid before her first furlough was rightly due. It would not only be the poorest kind of missionary economy to ask her to do her own work and look after her family herself, but it would be almost criminal to allow her to do it. At the same time, there are always worthy native men and women, some of whom have lost their all by their profession of Christianity, who, for a very small stipend are ready to serve the missionary and earn an honest living while doing something to further the cause of Christ. There are many missionaries' servants who serve the missionaries for a far smaller sum than they could get if they would serve foreigners who are not engaged in Christian work, or local officials who would gladly pay them more for the services they can render. They regard themselves in no small measure as missionaries, too, and are ready to sacrifice in their wages in order that they may be connected with the aggressive Christian work. Many of these servants are real forces for righteousness in the community.

Then, too, the influence on the native community is greater if the missionary lives in something of the style of his home land, and thus by his living, lifts up the home life of the people all around him. As the missionary home is the center of his activities, it is constantly visited by multitudes of people from all over the country, and they observe most carefully the home and its surroundings, as well as the relations existing between the husband and wife. The influence of the home, therefore, as it extends over the country, is only second to that of the missionary as a preacher and a teacher of righteousness. The home influence is unbounded as it is exerted over the various nationalities of the Oriental world.

Another reason why it is essential that the missionary should maintain his home in an orderly way is that his children are Western children and not Orientals. They are entitled to be surrounded by some little touches of Western life, and not to grow up in foreign countries with foreign surroundings so that when they come home for their education they will be in most respects foreign. They remain Occidental children, and, although a large number of them later enter the missionary work, they enter it as Westerners, who, although born abroad, have been reared in Western influences and under Christian training in civilized homes, where the strength and judgment of their character was formed in early childhood. The orderly, Christian, Western home is proving itself to be best adapted to the life of the missionary, not only for his immediate influence upon the people, but for the permanent influences that lead to the Christianization of those lands.

Some missionaries have attempted to live as the people live, discarding all appearances of their Western training, and living as the natives. Almost every such effort has ignominiously failed. The missionary who attempted it has broken down in health, and at the same time has failed to influence the people whom he hoped to reach by the process. The Occidental is known everywhere to be an Occidental, and the natives despise him if he pretends, by the way he lives, that he is something else. None are quicker to detect the sham than the people themselves.

The question is raised why, occasionally, visitors who go to the mission field bring back such unfavorable reports of the manner in which the missionaries live. This question has been partially answered by what has already been said, that is, that the traveler expects to find the missionary living in squalor, like the natives, and is surprised to find a clean, tasteful, orderly, comfortable home in which the missionary finds peace and rest, and from which he goes to his arduous duties. The disappointment is sometimes so great that the traveler reports that the missionary is living in luxury and squandering the money that is given for his missionary work.

Another reason is that always when a guest from the West or the home land honors the missionary with a visit, the very best that the missionary home can afford is brought forward. Sometimes it is a rare occurrence for a missionary, far in the interior of a foreign country, to have the privilege of entertaining a fellow countryman. It is most natural that the good housewife should do her best to conceal any hardships or deprivations with which she may contend ordinarily, and put before the guest the very best that the house can afford. Some years ago, an Englishman, a scientist of no little renown, visited one of the mission fields of a mission society, and went at once as guest to the home of a resident missionary. The missionary and his wife felt highly honored that so distinguished a man should visit them, and everything was done for his comfort. Almost every missionary home has canned goods which have been brought out from America or from England, and are kept against time of special emergency, possibly famine, generally sickness. This missionary had no guest room. The husband and wife gave the distinguished visitor their own room, and slept in an outhouse, upon straw, in most uncomfortable surroundings. For two weeks or more this man of science remained the guest of these missionaries, and went away hardly expressing his thanks for the entertainment he had received. After his return to England, he published an article in an English paper accusing the missionaries of living in great luxury, and giving as an illustration his own experience, naming the missionary whose guest he had been. The case was carefully investigated, and the facts as stated above were brought to light. This is, perhaps, a fair illustration of many of the severe criticisms that have been made of the luxuriousness of missionary living. Every such case, as reported, should be investigated, in order that the exact facts may be known. There is no reason why the manner in which any missionary lives should not be investigated and given the widest publicity.

The salaries paid missionaries, if investigation is

made, prove beyond any possibility of a doubt that they do not live in luxury unless they have other sources of support than their salary. There are a few missionaries who have personal resources upon which they can draw, but it is a known fact that few of them do draw upon their resources in order that they may live in a manner better than their associates who are entirely dependent upon the salaries paid them by the missionary society. They are all agreed that the missionary should not live in luxury, and they are practically agreed as to how he shall live. The salaries are small, even if they were measured by the expenses in this country. In many instances the missionary has to pay Western prices for necessaries of life, to which is added from thirty to fifty per cent. for import duty and transportation to the place where he is at work. In some of our mission fields this makes the same article cost the missionary much more than it does the worker in America or in England. It is equally true that whatever can be purchased in the country usually costs less than if purchased at home and sent out. A large part of most missionaries supplies must come from home.

There is no mission board, and no missionary family, and no missionary, who would not be willing to have their style of life and expenses carefully investigated by anyone who wishes to inquire into them. There is no doubt that such an inquiry, if made known to the public, would entirely allay any criticism which may be offered by those who feel that the missionaries' life is too luxurious. In spite of these luxuries which have been charged against the missionary, we do not find that young men and young women are offering themselves for service in sufficient numbers to fill the vacancies on the mission field and meet the demands for enlargement. Every one who offers himself for service to the mission board does so with the distinct understanding that he is to work for his simple living from year to year, without any possibility of his laying up anything for old age, or against sickness in the future. He receives only what he will need from month to month, trusting the future to God. It is hard to charge such people with luxurious living, and with wasting money which is given for missionary work. I venture the statement that, if one goes the world over, he will not find a class of people who are more economical in their expenditures, who endeavor in every way in their power to make every dollar count for the most in the advancement of the Kingdom of God, and who are so forgetful of their own personal interests and desires, as the foreign missionaries who have given up their home life and have identified themselves, so long as God shall give them strength to work, with the people to whom they have been sent, and for whose elevation, Christianization, and civilization they are laboring.

ILLUSTRATIVE QUOTATIONS

1. *Mr. R. E. Bredon:* "I can say that the conduct of the missionaries was, in my opinion, not only creditable, but admirable. All that went to make our life moderately comfortable and safe was done by missionaries or under

their auspices. The helpfulness and unselfishness shown by the missionary ladies, many of whom had the burdens of heavy family cares of their own to bear, were beyond praise."

2. *C. D. Hartranft, D. D., LL. D., President Hartford Theological Seminary:* "Nor less efficient and inclusive are the services of foreign missions in the introduction of new or in the modification of existing forces that are instrumental in developing the social order. For who inculcates a higher ideal than the missionary, of the present life and of the methods by which that ideal shall be most carefully preserved and advanced? Who has a better philosophy of the body, in that he views our physical framework as the divinely ordained instrument of righteousness?"

3. *Ho Yo, Chinese Consular General:* "The missionaries in China are high-minded, self-sacrificing men and women, willing to undergo infinite personal inconvenience in the hope and effort of bettering the spiritual and material conditions of others; and there is no question that among all the foreigners, the Chinese have their most steadfast and self-abnegating friends among the missionaries. The good they have conferred upon China cannot be estimated, for most of the foreign educational work which has gone on in China has been at their hands. They have introduced the Western literature; learning our language, as they aptly and quietly do, they become translaters into Chinese of Western books, and with them start schools for the instruction of the youth in the new fields of thought."

4. *Sir Harry H. Johnston:* "No person who desires

to make a truthful statement can deny the great good effected by missionary enterprise in Central Africa. There are some missions and some missionaries out here of whose work nothing but praise can be uttered, though much just criticism might be written on their mode of life, which in some instances is singularly and needlessly ascetic and uncomfortable."

5. *Hon. James Bryce, M.P.*: "I cannot mention the American missionaries without a tribute to the admirable work they have done. They have been the only good influence that has worked from abroad upon the Turkish Empire. They have shown great judgment and tact in their relations with the ancient churches of the land, Orthodox, Gregorian, Jacobite, Nestorian, and Catholic. They have lived cheerfully in the midst, not only of hardships, but latterly of serious dangers also. They have been the first to bring the light of education and learning into these dark places, and have rightly judged that it was far better to diffuse that light through their schools than to aim at a swollen roll of converts. From them alone, if we except the British consuls, has it been possible during the last thirty years to obtain trustworthy information regarding what passes in the interior."

6. *Dr. Robert N. Cust*: "The missionary appears to me to be the highest type of human excellence in the nineteenth century, and his profession to be the noblest. He has the enterprise of the merchant without the narrow desire for gain: the dauntlessness of the soldier, without the shedding of blood: the zeal of the geographical explorer, but from higher motives than science.

"The missionaries to Africa have sacrificed careers which might have been great and honored in their own countries, and gone forth to live in hovels and sometimes to die. The scholars of German universities have rejoiced exceedingly at the wonderful, unexpected, and epoch-making results of their quiet labors."

7. *President Charles Cuthbert Hall, D. D., Haskell Lecturer to India:* "I have traveled from one end of India to the other, have visited missions in every presidency representing American and British efforts, have inspected institutions, studied methods, and observed the spirit of the workers. The result of my observations is increased respect for missionaries and admiration for their work.

"There is nothing to criticise, as well as nothing to conceal, in the manner of life of our leading missionaries. The splendid devotion to duty, the abundance and willingness of their labors, their statesman-like grasp upon the problems with which they are dealing, at once humble and inspire men of open and honest minds who are permitted as guests to tarry beneath their roofs. And as for the scale of living which they maintain and which, be it remembered, is maintained upon an income wholly out of proportion to the magnitude of the interests that they represent, it is to be said that they exhibit a sense of propriety, an appreciation of the fitness of things for which they deserve gratitude only. The refinement of their home life is one of the elements of their Christian influence. Their manner of living harmonizes with the work that they do and with the relations that they sustain to the community at large. It is to be hoped that the coarse and shallow criticisms which from time to time have gained circulation in America touching the ease and luxury of missionary households henceforth may be discredited. After having been permitted to sojourn in the homes of scores of missionaries in all parts of India, in Ceylon, and in Japan, it is an honor to testify that there has been observed only that which illustrates good sense, the consecrated use of opportunity, and wise and helpful self-adjustment to the environment."

8. *George H. Hepworth, editor and author:* " My purpose is twofold: first to show the American people the kind of work in which the missionaries in Turkey are engaged, and second to assure them from personal observation that these missionaries do not encourage revolutionists or the revolutionary spirit. I am surer of nothing than I am of this. If you could see them at their somewhat thankless tasks you would regard them as the most consecrated men and women on the planet, as far removed from fostering rebellion as heaven is from the earth, making the sacrifice of life and of all social and even domestic relations, and doing it with a cheerfulness which must command not only our respect but also our admiration.

" The price to be paid for the enlightenment of the nation is very heavy, but these noble men and saintly women are willing to pay it, and I, for one, feel that my poor life amounts to nothing in comparison, so with a full heart, a heart with a big ache in it, I cry, ' God bless them ! '

" The missionaries are the Sir Knights of modern times, their weapons are no longer swords, but ideas. They are to be found in all quarters of the globe, and they are always surrounded by ambushed perils. They are the representatives of a high civilization and of the best religious thought of the age, and are the ' little leaven ' which in good time is to ' leaven the whole lump.' I do not hesitate to say they are doing more for the Turkey of to-day than all the European Powers combined."

9. *Lord John Lawrence, Viceroy of India:* "Notwithstanding all that the English people have done to benefit that country, the missionaries have done more than all other agencies combined. They have had arduous and uphill work, often receiving no encouragement, and sometimes a great deal of discouragement, from their own countrymen, and have had to bear the taunts and obloquy of those who despised and disliked their preaching, but such has been the effect of their earnest zeal, untiring devotion, and of the excellent example which they have, I may say, universally shown to the people, that I have no doubt whatever that, in spite of the great masses of the people being intensely opposed to their doctrine, they are, as a body, remarkably popular in the country.

"I have a great reverence and regard for them [the missionaries] both personally and for the sake of the great cause in which they are engaged, and I feel it to be a pleasure and a privilege to do anything I can in the last years of my life to further the great work for which they have done so much."

10. *George F. Hoar, United States Senator for Massachusetts:* "In this day of our pride and exultation at the deeds of our young heroes in Manila and Cuba, let us not forget that the American missionary in the paths of peace belongs to the same heroic stock and is an example of the same heroic temper.

"I have regretted to hear in this debate some sneers at the missionaries, and the sons of missionaries, who have redeemed Hawaii and who are presenting her at the gates of the people of the United States. There is not a story of true heroism or true glory in human annals which can surpass the story of missionaries to this or in foreign lands whom America has sent as the servants of civilization and piety."

11. *Secretary for India:* "The government of India can not but acknowledge the great obligation under which it is laid by the benevolent exertions made by the missionaries whose blameless examples and self-denying labors have infused new vigor into the stereotyped life of the great population placed under English rule."

12. *Charles S. Smith, Esq., in the New York "Tribune":* "I have visited the stirring scenes of the Indian mutiny at Lucknow, Cawnpore, and Delhi. I have stood reverently and with uncovered head beside the graves of Havelock and Lawrence. I have read the tablets of Lord Napier, upon which he inscribed the names of the gallant men who carried the Kashmir gate by storm, and gave their lives to save the honor and the empire of the English race in India. I solemnly believe that no soldier, who (in Lawrence's last words) died trying to do his duty, has deserved better of his country and of mankind than have those brave men and women of the Madura mission, who face daily the fever of the jungle and cholera, which is always present in India, and are, with heroic self-sacrifice, wearing out their lives silently for the good of others."

13. *The "Hindu," India:* "The missionaries' simple lives, their sympathy with the poor, their self-sacrifice, all force admiration from their critics."

MISSIONARY AND LUXURIOUS LIVING

14. *James B. Angell, LL.D., President of the University of Michigan, and formerly United States Minister to China and Turkey:* "I have had the good fortune to be in the homes of princes and the palaces of the rich in many lands, but I am speaking the simple truth when I say that I have never been anywhere in the world in homes which impressed me so with the happiness of the dwellers as the humble homes of our hard-working missionaries on the foreign field. It was not the happiness of pomp, but it was that highest of all earthly happiness, which God grants to every man and every woman who makes the supreme end and desire of life to do the work of the Master, regardless of personal comfort."

X

THE MISSIONARY AND HIS ACHIEVEMENTS

ONE frequently hears the statement made that missionaries have accomplished practically nothing, and have made no real impression upon foreign countries. Probably the foundation for such a statement is the remarks of the round-the-world traveler, who has visited many different countries and remained several days in some of the large port cities in which mission boards report large operations, and he distinctly says that he " saw nothing of any kind of mission work." The writer spent five months and more in Ceylon and India. In that time he traveled over 6000 miles on the railroads, in carriages and ox-carts and on foot. He traversed plains and jungles, skirted rice fields, climbed mountains by night and by day in southern India, in middle India, and in the north, and during all this time he was alert to see a venomous snake and to hear a tiger, or at least see his tracks. But he saw or heard neither the one nor the other. And yet government statistics report that some 30,000 people in that country die annually from snake bites and tiger attacks. It is undoubtedly true that not one out of a hundred foreign travelers in India ever sees a venomous reptile there except in captivity. Would these people venture to assert upon this evidence that there are no snakes or tigers in India? The argument against missions based upon, " I did not see any mission work in any of those countries," is just as valuable as the statement, "I did not see a single snake in India " would be against the existence of such reptiles there. Both exist, and the proof of this statement is abundant and incontrovertible. An argument based upon ignorance is not of much weight, when put over against the argument of demonstrable facts.

Missionaries have achieved some things that are so patent to all who will observe, that little ground remains for questioning. A few of the marked achievements of the last century are the following:

(1) *They have intrenched and fortified themselves in all the strategic centers of the non-Christian world.* In any great movement, it is of primary importance to gain strategic positions. It was for this that Japan and Russia contended in the recent war. Much of the international controversy of the world arises over questions gathering about the occupancy of strategic points. When a nation commands such a position, it reckons the victory as practically won. There are to-day in every large city and important town in Japan, China, Korea, Africa, India, Ceylon, Burmah, Turkey, and many other countries, Christian missionary plants, many of long standing, and most of them thoroughly established as a part of the country itself. These mission plants extend far beyond the cities, and cover vast regions of country where all organized opposition has ceased, and the Christian missionary is freely accorded

every liberty. A century ago, hardly a door was open in any foreign land, and hardly a foothold had been gained anywhere.

These plants include not only missionary residences owned by mission boards, but school plants of every grade and order, hospitals, dispensaries, printing and publishing establishments, churches, orphan asylums, rescue homes, leper asylums, industrial plants, and in fact every kind of institution that exemplifies and advances Christianity in this country. These are found, in whole or in part, in every large center of the non-Christian world, and some of them in towns of importance in the remote interior districts of most of the mission countries. Many of these institutions have become so much a part of the life and thought of the people themselves that they are hardly thought of as "missionary institutions," but are reckoned as belonging to the native Christian community.

In the city of Tokyo, in Japan, there are to-day some ninety Christian churches, with which there are connected over fifty branches where regular Christian services are conducted. It would require from one to three weeks, or even more, for a person to visit every distinctive Christian institution in any one of the large centers of the non-Christian world, and give each even the most cursory observation. The possession by Christian missions of these strategic points in the conquest of the world is an achievement of importance which cannot be measured by any standards we possess. For proof of the existence of these institutions of Christianity, see Beach's " Geography and Atlas of

Missions," or Dennis's " Christian Missions and Social Progress." Even these do not record the large number of native Christian institutions which are the direct results of missionary operations.

(2) *Modern education has been introduced into most if not all of the non-Christian countries by the missionaries.* This is conspicuously true of China, Siam, India, Persia, Turkey, and Africa. A generation of missionary effort was necessary in most cases to convince the people in these lands of the value of an education, and another generation to persuade them to be willing to support in a large measure their own schools. Persistently and patiently, the missionaries have adhered to the idea that the Christian church can never be permanently established among a people living in dense ignorance. No one to-day can take even a cursory survey of the great number of colleges and higher institutions of learning and the multitude of lower schools which these necessitated, all established by the missionaries or growing directly out of their work, filled with the brightest and best young men and women in every non-Christian country of the world, and not be overwhelmed with a sense of the marvelous achievement. These schools, with their instruction in modern sciences and in the English language, and their insistence upon the Anglo-Saxon conception of Christian integrity, justice, and truth, are doing more for peace and unity in the world than the united navies of Christendom.

These educational institutions include kindergartens and all grades of schools, which in many cases have become the models after which government schools have been patterned. The kindergarten, now so popular in Japan, was begun and fostered by missionaries, who have prepared much of the literature now used in government schools. The model orphan asylum, now recognized as such by the Japanese government, was a missionary asylum. The first nurses' training school for Japanese girls was a missionary training school, whose graduates soon made a name for themselves in the empire. The missionary primary, intermediate, and normal schools in Ceylon and India have so met the approbation of the local governments that large appropriations are annually made from government funds for their support. The first schools for the modern education of girls in most of these countries were missionary schools. These have greatly multiplied, and have become in many cases the models for national schools.

The missionary collegiate institutions are unique and exceedingly powerful. They are to be found in every important country, and their students and graduates are holding positions of responsibility and trust in every land. In these the English language is the only available common tongue, and all graduates are compelled to become in a large measure masters of English. There are few of these colleges in which students of numerous nationalities are not represented. They are all eager to learn English. Robert College at Constantinople has usually not less than a dozen nationalities among its students, each race with its own distinctive tongue. The same thing is true in a measure of most of the colleges in Turkey and of many in India, China, Africa, Siam, and other countries. The educational systems of many of these countries are being shaped by the men and women who are trained in these mission institutions.

(3) *Missionaries have created a modern literature for most of the non-Christian peoples.* Throughout Africa, the Pacific islands, India, Turkey, Bulgaria, China, and Japan, and in many other countries, there was either no vernacular literature in any form, or none that was modern in its content and character, until the missionaries created it through the Bible translated, and schoolbooks and other publications. The Bible, through not a few of those earlier translations, has done perhaps even more for the purification of the native spoken language and its preservation and unification than Luther's Bible did for the German tongue, and our King James Version for the English. Through these efforts, there are to-day no people of great numbers who do not possess the beginnings, at least, of a modern vernacular literature, and in some countries, like Japan, the people themselves have caught the spirit of the age, and are abundantly sustaining the work. The literature provided, besides that which is distinctly religious, includes periodicals of broad scope and influence, and school and scientific books of every grade. The annual output of the brains and presses of the mission field to-day in the vernacular of the peoples among whom the work is carried on amounts to more than one million pages a day.

In contemplating the importance of this Christian

literature, we should bear in mind the awakening intelligence of these peoples through mission and government schools, increasing rapidly in every mission country. The statement made above of the output of mission presses and the product of the pens of missionaries and Christian natives does not include the great work carried on in this line by native Christian editors of secular papers. Not less than five of the leading dailies of Japan are edited by well-known Christian Japanese. Leading editorials upon Christian themes are constantly found in their columns. In addition to all this, the native Christian writer is making himself known in many of these different countries and in a great variety of ways. Sometimes this is in the form of special articles in non-Christian publications, and sometimes as Christian stories published independently and sold in the open market. The value and far-reaching influence of this literary output is beyond computation. It includes every language that has been reduced to writing, and to-day reaches nearly every man, woman, and child who can read his own tongue. It reaches beyond the borders, where the missionary himself cannot go, and is read in secret where the reader would scorn to be seen listening to the Christian preacher. Its influence is silent but potent, undemonstrative but far-reaching, fundamental and permanent.

(4) *A vast army of native Christian literary and educational workers have been trained and put into the work.* At the beginning, all missionary work was necessarily carried on by missionaries from abroad.

To-day, foreigners represent but a small fraction of the working force. The pastors of the native churches, the evangelists and aggressive force in the field, the rank and file of the teachers in the native schools, the majority of those producing the vernacular literature, are trained natives who are demonstrating their ability to do this work by their manifest capacity for leadership among their own people. All this is transforming the modern mission movement from a foreign innovation into a domestic organization. The native organizations have reached different degrees of development, according as the people have shown capacity for education and leadership. But the one principle has been established, that the chief duty of the foreign missionary is to raise up, develop, and install in the work trained native Christians who shall ultimately become the only leaders in the rapidly forming Christian society. As an illustration to show how this work has developed under the American Board, it is sufficient to state that for every ordained missionary in its twenty missions to-day, there are twenty-one native Christian workers.

In 1850 the American Board had nearly as many male missionaries on the field as it has to-day. Then there were but 122 trained native Christian workers, while now in connection with its twenty missions there are more than four thousand Christian natives who are pastors, preachers, and teachers of their people, and the true leaders in every form of Christian work. The plan of the campaign of the Kingdom contemplates the raising up of the army of conquest in the country to be conquered, and then to secure from the country itself the support of that army. Already many of these native workers receive their full support from the people themselves. Many of these leaders are organizing and putting into operation native missionary, educational, and benevolent societies, sustained by native contributions and directed by local talent. Many of these societies have already proven their strength and usefulness by the important work they are doing in the line of extending Christian institutions of every character into regions beyond the point yet reached by the foreign missionary effort. This work, backed by the independent native church, constitutes the crown and glory of missionary operations.

(5) *Foreign missions have largely revolutionized the Oriental ideas of womanhood.* The general, original conception was that woman's highest function was to be the servant or slave of man, and that she was unworthy or incapable of receiving an education. We find now, in every mission country in the world, not only mission schools for girls, filled with pupils, but we see also native or national schools for girls of varying grades and proficiency in those same countries. While the education of girls in all these countries has not kept pace with that of boys, yet there are now in many places large and flourishing national schools for girls supported by the government or by private funds and crowded with pupils. A deep sentiment in favor of educating girls, and a decidedly changed conception in many countries as to the relations of women to society, mark the stages of the emancipation of Oriental

womanhood from a life of servitude to one of large service. In Japan, women lead in the Red Cross work and in national organizations for the protection of the purity of the home. In India educated native women are banded together in efforts to better the condition of child widows, and in China to abolish foot binding. In Turkey cultivated and trained women are demonstrating their power to revolutionize the social life of the country. The pure, refined, Christian home, the women occupying positions of leadership in native society, an extended and almost world-wide movement for the general education of girls, and the completed women's organizations which are already producing reforms of the social life of all mission countries, demonstrate the operations of an established force for the social regeneration of the Orient.

(6) *Missions illustrate the power of God and the wisdom of God.* Protestant missionaries have gone out in the spirit of the Master, without the support of arms or armies, and with no political prestige or backing. They have not violently forced themselves into any country, and have not appealed to arms to maintain them there when once they have entered. They have been poor as far as earthly wealth is concerned, without sufficient funds to meet the immediate demands of the work. They have been but a handful of men and women compared with the multitudes to whom they were sent, and who were largely arrayed against them, and they have been compelled to face the deepest prejudice and the wildest superstitions. And yet, they have generally won their way, in the face of

indifference at times, and often of violent and bloody persecution, gaining the confidence of the people, until mighty Christian institutions have been established, the ideas of multitudes radically changed upon religious and moral subjects, and the foundations laid for the formation of a new society. The foreign missionary movement has demonstrated itself to be the most successful and most important movement of the age, producing the largest and most permanent results from the minimum expenditure of money and life.

Even a cursory survey of the story of missions during the last century will reveal the mighty obstacles that presented themselves at the beginning, which have now almost, if not quite, disappeared. The heat of the conflict is over, and now the Christian Church must settle itself down to the question of combination, better organization, and the development of resources that exist so abundantly, both at home and in the foreign countries themselves. These resources are measured at present more in terms of men than of money. The church at home should provide funds in far larger amounts than at present, in order that the positions already won may not be lost, and that an advance commensurate with present achievements may be made.

The student volunteer movement has aroused the young men and women of our universities and colleges. More of them are now systematically studying missions than at any other period in the history of the world. Their very numbers constitute a challenge to the churches to provide the means to send them abroad as soon as they are ready to go. The number of student volunteers is rapidly increasing. There must be a corresponding increase in the gifts of those who cannot go. This great army of the best men and women of our higher educational institutions enlisted in the service of foreign missions is the grandest of all achievements, and is the assurance under God of complete victory.

ILLUSTRATIVE QUOTATIONS

1. *James B. Angell, LL. D., President of the University of Michigan, and formerly United States Minister to China and Turkey:* "I want to say, once for all, that after perhaps somewhat exceptional opportunities for observing the mission, not only of our Board [American Board of Commissioners for Foreign Missions] but of the Boards of our Presbyterian, Baptist, Methodist, and Episcopal brethren in China, and also the Boards of the European Churches, I come fully prepared to say, as my own conviction, that the work of foreign missions is now planted upon so solid a foundation, and gives so much promise in that hardest of all fields that we till, China, that there is nothing left for us but to push on to the glorious end which every believer in this Word of God must feel assured awaits us at the last."

2. *Bishop Charles B. Galloway, D. D.:* "I do not think that Theodore Parker was extravagant when he said, 'If the whole missionary work had accomplished no more than the building up of one such character as Adoniram Judson, it would be worth all it cost.' What

names to-day are written in largest letters in the story of Africa, about which we are reading so much? Not those who guide the affairs of government, not those who carry the flag of their country in triumph, but the names of Robert Moffatt and of David Livingstone. In India, viceroys and generals may be forgotten, Hastings and Lord Clive and the rest, but Carey and Schwartz and Marshman and Reginald Heber and Edward Parker and scores of others shine resplendent as the very stars of heaven."

3. *Sir W. Muir:* "Thousands have been brought over, and in an ever-increasing ratio converts are being brought over to Christianity. And they are not shams, not paper converts, as some would have us believe, but good and honest Christians, and many of them of a high standard."

4. *Professor Silliman of Yale University:* "It would be impossible for the historians of the islands of the Pacific to ignore the important contributions of American missionaries to science."

5. *John Quincy Adams, President of the United States:* "It is a subject of cheering contemplation to the friends of human improvement and virtue that, by the mild and gentle influence of Christian charity, dispensed by humble missionaries of the gospel, unarmed with secular power, within the last quarter of a century, the people of this group of islands [the Hawaiian] have been converted from the lowest abasement of idolatry to the blessings of the Christian gospel; united under one balanced government; rallied to the fold of civilization by a written language and constitution providing security for the rights of persons, property, and mind, and invested with

all the elements of right and power which can entitle them to be acknowledged by their brethren of the human race as a separate and independent community."

6. *Professor Christlieb of Bonn University:* "The Bible ideas of self-respect, the foundations of all true culture, are dispelling the long night of heathen degradation."

7. *Mr. J. J. Jackson, Magistrate of Natal, South Africa:* "Mission work in South Africa is undoubtedly successful. I have come in contact with many of your converts who are a credit to any community, people who are leading quiet, industrious, and respectable lives, and as far as I can judge, lives actuated by Christian principle. These people are, I have no hesitation in saying, exerting a beneficial influence on those around them, an influence which is bound, sooner or later, to make itself felt upon those who at present make no professions of Christianity."

[Among the visible results of labors among the natives, this magistrate mentions "a substantial increase of marriages by Christian rites, instead of heathen ceremonies. It gives me great pleasure to testify this. I firmly believe that it is only a matter of time, when under the quiet, unostentatious work of the missionaries, polygamy will die out. The number of licenses issued by me during 1902 for marriages by Christian rites was double that for the previous year, which is a very encouraging fact and one which speaks well for the future of the natives. If this continues, as I believe it will, I see no reason why the much-vexed question of polygamy should not be solved by a natural process.]

"All credit is due to the missionaries who have succeeded in wisely placing before the natives the advisability of such marriages, and I am convinced that they will do more to abolish the practice of polygamy than any legislation on the part of Parliament can do. It is a remarkable fact that so few natives who have contracted Christian marriages break their marriage vows, prosecution of natives for bigamy being comparatively rare, as the records of our courts will show."

Mr. Jackson further says: "Another perceptible result of the labors of the missionaries is the appearance around their stations of neat little homesteads and gardens, the adoption of European methods of agriculture and of dress, and a general air of thriftiness, which is conspicuous by its absence among the raw natives."

8. *William Fleming Stevenson:* "These hundred years of modern missions have placed the Bible within intelligible reach of perhaps 500,000,000 of the race. Their light has gone out through all the earth, their words to the world's end. We see the plans of God unrolled before our eyes. And what are they? That the whole world may be touched by the Gospel: that it may not only touch the individual, but penetrate the tribal life and the national life in every place, and mould the proudest and most populous races by its teaching."

9. *Colonel Charles Denby, LL. D., United States Minister to China:* "The missionaries are the writers of books for the Chinese. They are the interpreters for them and the legations. They fight the demon, opium. About their religious work I have only this to say, that he who teaches Christianity teaches modern civilization. Depreciation, caviling, and sneering will disappear and the missionaries will stand before the world as they ought to stand—as

benefactors of the people among whom their lives are spent, and forerunners of the commerce of the world."

10. *Commodore Erskine, in a report to the Governor of New South Wales, said:* " The work done for the natives of New Guinea by the missionaries is so noble in its beneficent influence that no words of mine could exaggerate its praise—an influence that any crowned head might be proud to exercise over any people."

11. *Dr. Kane, Arctic explorer:* " The missionaries have been so far successful among the natives of Greenland that there are but few of them who are not now Christians. Before missionaries came, murder, burial of the living, and infanticide were not considered crimes. It was unsafe for vessels to touch upon the coast; but now Greenland is safer for the wrecked mariner than many parts of our own coast."

12. *Prince Malcolm Khan, Persian Minister:* "I have always considered the presence of your missionaries in Persia as a providential blessing. I do not speak of their religious mission, but of the admirable and far more praiseworthy efforts which they make to shed the light of European education throughout the entire East. I can assure you, moreover, that the eminently liberal spirit of his Majesty the Shah, and the intelligent men who are now his counsellors, fully appreciate the value of the services rendered by your worthy countrymen to the cause of civilization in Persia."

13. *Mr. Saunders, Chief Commissioner of Zululand:* " On my knowledge I can say that missionaries are try-

ing to do what no one else will do, and are altering the character of the natives. I do not know of any power that will do this but the power of Christianity."

14. *The "Geographer Meiniche" is quoted by Warneck, in "Missions and Culture," as saying,* "It is scarcely possible to deny the extraordinary importance of the missionary efforts of our time; they are yet really in their infancy; yet it is certain that they will wholly transform the nature and the relations of the non-Christian peoples, and will thereby produce one of the most magnificent and most colossal revolutions that human history contains."

15. *The Nineteenth Century:* "If the immediate success of British missions in spreading their religion over barbarous Africa be doubtful, it is consoling to reflect on the immense service which missionary enterprise has rendered Africa, to the world at large, and to Great Britain in particular. . . . It is a force which has effected greater changes for the better in the condition of savage Africa than armies and navies, conferences and treaties have yet done."

16. *Editor of a Japan daily paper:* "Look all over Japan. Our forty millions have a higher standard of morality than they have ever known. There is not a boy or girl throughout the empire that has not heard of the one-man-one-woman doctrine. Our ideas of loyalty and obedience are higher than ever. And when we inquire the cause of this great moral advance, we can find it in nothing else than the religion of Jesus."

17. *W. L. Watkinson, Editor of the "London Quarterly Review":* "Really our missionary enterprise, the

198

missionary enterprise of the Church of God in England, is the very salt of our civilization. WHEREIN LIES OUR SAFETY? In spiritual magnanimity! If you want to take care of your empire take care of your missions. It is a strange thing to say, but guarantee for your splendour is your sacrifice. You are going to keep your wealth just as you give it away in noble causes. The tonic for your luxury is the generosity that does and dares for the perishing; and if you want to keep your place with the topmost nations, you will keep your place at the top by taking a tremendous stoop to those who are at the base. And so this morning, if you want to take care of your empire, see to it that you take care of the orphan and the slave and the barbarian; and if you want to put a ring of fire round the grandest civilization that this world has ever seen, put a belt of mission stations round your empire, and your empire is safe until the millennium."

18. *Rear Admiral Geo. E. Belknap, United States Navy:* "I assert it to be a fact beyond contradiction that there is not a ruler, official, merchant, or any other person, from emperors, viceroys, judges, governors, counsellors, generals, ministers, admirals, merchants, and others down to the lowest coolies in China and Japan, Siam and Korea, who, in their associations or dealings with their fellowmen in that quarter of the globe are not indebted every day of their lives to the work and achievements of the American missions."

19. *J. Dyer Ball, Esq., Hong Kong:* "Had Protestant missionaries done nothing else in China than prepare and publish the books issued by them in Chinese: start the schools: written the books in English, containing nar-

ratives of their own travels, and accounts of the natives, and of their religious customs and manners: translated native works: instructed the youth of both sexes, and founded hospitals and dispensaries—had these, we say, been the only things accomplished by Protestant missionaries, they would have done a noble work; but added to all these more secular labors is the directly religious work of preaching the gospel, that and Bible distribution, visiting, gathering together the converts, etc., all of which, though less appreciated by the general mercantile community of China, has been as signally successful as the other class of undertakings."

20. *Henry Drummond, scientist, traveler, author:* "If one saw a single navvy trying to remove a mountain, the desolation of the situation would be appalling. Most of us have seen a man or two, or a hundred or two ministers, missionaries, Christian layman—at work upon the higher evolution of the world: but it is when one sees them by the thousands in every land, and every tongue, and the mountain honeycombed and slowly crumbling, on each of its frowning sides, that the majesty of the missionary work fills and inspires the mind."

21. *Hon. Richard H. Dana, in an article reporting observations on the Hawaiian Islands in* 1860: "It is no small thing to say of the missionaries of the American Board that, in less than forty years they have taught this whole people [the Hawaiians] to read and to write, to cipher and to sew. They have given them an alphabet, grammar and dictionary, preserved their language from extinction, given it a literature, and translated into it the Bible and works of devotion, science, entertainment, etc. They have established schools, reared up native teachers,

and so pressed their work that now the proportion of inhabitants who can read and write is greater than in New England."

22. *Sir William Hunter, author of the "Imperial Gazetteer" of India:* " The record of the work done by the first missionaries in India reads like an Eastern romance. They created a prose literature for Bengal: they established the modern method of popular education: they founded the present Protestant Indian church: they gave the first impulse to the native press: they set up the first steam engine in India: with its help they introduced the modern manufacture of paper on a large scale: in ten years they translated and printed the Bible, or parts thereof, in thirty-one languages. The main part of their funds they earned by their own hands and heads. They built a college which still ranks among the most splendid educational edifices in India."

23. *Babu Keshub Chunder Sen:* " The many noble deeds of philanthropy and self-denying benevolence which Christian missionaries have performed in India, and the various intellectual, social, and moral improvements which they have effected, need no flattering comment: they are treasured in the gratitude of the nation, and can never be forgotten or denied. That India is highly indebted to these large-hearted followers of Christ for her present prosperity, I have no doubt the entire nation will gratefully acknowledge.

" The missionaries have brought unto us Christ. They have given us the high code of Christian ethics, and their teaching and example have secretly influenced and won thousands of non-Christian Hindus.

" The spirit of Christianity has already pervaded the

whole atmosphere of Indian society, and we breathe, think, feel, and move in a Christian atmosphere. Native society is being aroused, enlightened, and reformed under the influence of Christian education."

24. *Sir Charles Elliott:* "The growth of Christianity in India has been a solid fact, and sufficiently rapid to give all needful encouragement to the supporters of missions. Now this being the case, it will seem at first sight very strange that so many residents in India should be ignorant of what is going on under their eyes, and that we should so frequently hear their sneers and cavils at the small results of missionary effort. The simple explanation is to be found, I believe, in the extremely narrow limits of our opportunities for observation, and these limits are mainly imposed by the excessive absorption of every one in his particular work or office."

25. *Tuan Fong, the Viceroy of Fukien, China, in the offices of the American Board said:* "It has been my pleasure to render some service to the missionaries of this Board myself during the late troubles in China. I want to say, without desiring to be partial in my judgment, that the missionaries of this Board have given the best results of any in the missionary field in my country by their display of tact, prudence, and good sense, all of which are so necessary to friendly intercourse of different nationalities. Send us more like these you have sent."

26. *Sir Bartle Frere, Governor of Bombay:* "Christianity has now been preached to fetish-worshipping tribes in every stage of civilization, and the invariable result

has been to show that Chrisianity has power to prevail against fetish worship, and that the results of the acceptance of Christianity by the fetish worshippers are invariably to raise him in the moral and social scale, and to make him a civilized being."

27. *Sir Herbert Edwardes, Major-General English army in India:* "I believe if the English were driven out of India to-morrow, Christianity would remain and triumph."

28. *Mr. Charles Darwin, naturalist:* "The lesson of the missionary is the enchanter's wand. The house has been built, the windows framed, the fields ploughed, and even the trees grafted by the New Zealander. When I looked at the whole scene, I thought it admirable. . . . I took leave of the missionaries with feelings of high respect for their useful, upright characters. I think it would be difficult to find a body of men better adapted for the high office which they fill. . . . The march of improvement consequent on the introduction of Christianity throughout the South Sea, probably stands by itself in the records of history."

"It appears to me that the morality and religion of the inhabitants are highly creditable. There are many who attacked both the missionaries, their system, and the effect produced by it. Such reasoners never compare the present state with that of the Island Tahiti only twenty years ago: nor even with that of Europe at the present day; but they compare it with the high standard of gospel perfection. Inasmuch as the condition of the people falls short of this high standard, blame is attached to the missionary instead of credit for that which he has effected. They forget, or will not remember, that human

sacrifices and the power of an idolatrous priesthood—
a system of profligacy unparalleled in any other part of
the world—infanticide a consequence of that system—
bloody wars, where the conquerors spared neither women
nor children—that all these have been abolished and that
dishonesty, intemperance, and licentiousness have been
greatly reduced, by the introduction of Christianity."

29. *Mr. William T. Stead, editor, author:* " How
many American citizens, I wonder, are aware that from
the slopes of Mount Ararat all the way to the shores of
the Blue Aegean Sea, American missionaries have scattered broadcast over all the distressful land the seed of
American principles. When General Mosseloff, the
director of foreign faiths within the Russian Empire,
visited Etchmiadzin, the Armenian patriarch, spread before him a map of Asia Minor, which was marked all
over with American colleges, American churches, American schools, American missions. They [the American
missionaries] are busy everywhere, teaching, preaching,
begetting new life in these Asiatic races."

30. *Thomas H. Norton, Ph. D., United States Consul
at Harpoot and Smyrna, Turkey:* " I have had occasion
to revert to the work of the accomplished and devoted
band of American missionaries and teachers settled in
these districts. In a thousand ways they are raising the
standard of morality, of intelligence, of education, of material well-being, of industrial enterprise. Directly or indirectly every phase of their work is rapidly paving the
way for American commerce. Special stress should be
laid upon the remarkable work of the physicians, ordained
or unordained, who are attached to the various stations.
They form a steadily growing network, dotting the map of

Asia Minor at Cesarea, Marsovan, Sivas, Adana, Aintab, Mardin, Harpoot, Bitlis, and Van. At most of these points well-equipped hospitals are in active operation. From the very nature of their occupation they come more easily and rapidly into touch with the Turkish population and quickly gain their confidence.

"Taking all in all, I regard the results following the foundation of this institution [Euphrates College] as among the most important and noteworthy secured by American effort in foreign lands. . . . The whole work appeals most strongly to one whose chief duty is to aid and further the entrance of American wares in this land. I know of no import better adapted to secure the future commercial supremacy of the United States in this land of such wonderful potential possibilities than the introduction of American teachers, of American educational appliances and books of American methods and ideas."

31. *Hon. Elisha H. Allen, Hawaiian Minister to the United States:* "I have a very high appreciation of the great work which the American Board has accomplished. No one can fully appreciate it unless by a visit to the country which has been blessed by its labors. It was a great triumph to have saved the nation and to have brought it within the family of nations, which was so important to Christian civilization and to the commerce of the world, and more especially of the United States."

32. *Sir W. Mackworth Young, late Lieutenant-Governor of the Punjab, India:* "The census reports of the last four decades show that the native Christian population of India has increased from one and one-fourth million in 1872 to two and three-fourth millions in 1901. During the last decade, while the general population in-

creased by one and one-half per cent., the native Christian population was increased by 30.8 per cent. 'The degree of success,' says the official census report, 'attending missionary effort at the present day is even greater than would appear from the rate of increase disclosed by these figures.' The Reformed Churches, which now number 845,000 converts, have increased since 1891 by forty-three per cent. In an article in the *Quarterly Review,* January, 1894, it was calculated that at the rate of progress then observed, the Protestant faith would absorb the entire population by the middle of the twenty-first century. Judged even by statistics, Christian missions are not a failure."

33. *William Fleming Stevenson:* "Within our generation China was inaccessible to the Gospel: Japan was impregnable: the heart of Africa was untrodden and unknown. Now, look a little deeper into the figures. It may be only a handful of missionaries at a single point, but they are translating the Bible, pouring Christian thought into the literature of a whole race.

"Almost the whole of Polynesia is Christian. Every coast of Africa is sieged. Greenland and Patagonia have their churches. The feet of them that publish the Gospel of Peace traverse the roads from the Himalaya to Cape Cormorin, from Burmah to the Yellow Sea. A survey of missions has become a survey of the world."

34. *Major Macdonald, British East Africa:* "Instead of a savage heathen kingdom, where a man's life was rated at the price of an ox, and a woman was an article of barter, and where justice went to the highest bidder, the Uganda of to-day is a well-ordered state, steadily improving in the arts of civilization and culture, where

no man can lose his property or his life at the arbitrary will of the great or without a fair and open trial. This alone is no small thing to have achieved, and a large share in its accomplishment is undoubtedly due to the patient toil of the Christian missionaries."

35. *Alexander McArthur, M. P.:* "I believe the advancement of civilization, the extension of commerce, the increase of knowledge in art, science, and literature, the promotion of civil and religious liberty, the development of countries rich in undiscovered mineral and vegetable wealth, are all intimately identified with, and to a much larger extent than most people are aware of, dependent upon the work of the missionary, and I hold that the missionary has done more to civilize and to benefit the heathen world than any or all other agencies ever employed."

INDEX

INDEX

I

ALPHABETICAL LIST OF AUTHORITIES QUOTED.

Roman numerals refer to chapters, and the arabic numerals to the number of the quotation within the chapter. As for instance, V 3 indicates the third quotation in chapter five.

211

AUTHORITIES QUOTED

Cooper, Mr. H. Stonehewer, III 16.

Currie, Sir Philip, British Ambassador to Constantinople, VIII 4.

Cust, Dr. Robert N., IX 6.

Curtis, William Eleroy, Correspondent, Author, and Traveler, IV 7.

Curzon, Lord, Viceroy of India, VIII 19.

Cutting, Mr. R. Fulton, New York, I 9.

Damrong, Prince, Minister of the Interior for Siam, VII 7.

Dana, Hon. Richard H., X 21.

Darwin, Charles, Naturalist, I 8. X 28.

Denby, Col. Charles, LL.D., for thirteen years United States Minister to China, I 15. III 21. V 15. VI 12. X 9.

Deputation of the A. B. C. F. M. to India and Ceylon, II 3.

Donovan, Mr. J. P., British officer in China, VI 13.

Drummond, Henry, Scientist, Traveler, and Author, X 20.

Dudgeon, Dr. John, thirty years resident in China, head of the Imperial College in Peking, Physician and Surgeon of the British and Japanese Legations in Peking, V 7.

Edward VII, King of Great Britain, VI 23.

Edwardes, Sir Herbert, Major-General of English Army in India, X 27.

Elliott, Sir Charles, X 24.

Erskine, Commodore, X 10.

Farrar, Archdeacon, VIII 14.

Field, Henry M., D. D., Editor New York Evangelist, III 7.

Fong, Tuan, Viceroy of Fukien, China, Special Commissioner to the United States, VII 30. X 25.

Forum, The, IV 5.

Foster, Hon. John W., Secretary of State, Diplomat, VI 15. VIII 20.

Fraser-Blair, Mr. A. J., Editor of the Englishman, VIII 18.

Frere, Sir Bartle, Governor of Bombay, V 1. X 26.

Fukuzawa, Mr., Editor of the Jiji Shimpo, Japan, IV 12.

THE MISSIONARY AND HIS CRITICS

AUTHORITIES QUOTED

AUTHORITIES QUOTED

AUTHORITIES CLASSIFIED

II

1. ARMY AND NAVY OFFICERS.

Belknap, Geo. E., Rear Admiral, United States Navy, X 18.

Donovan, Mr. J. P., British officer in China, VI 13.

Edwardes Sir Herbert, Major-General of English Army in India, X 27.

Erskine, Commodore, X 10.

Japanese, a commanding officer, VII 17.

Macdonald, Major, British East Africa, X 34.

Officer, an, who made a tour of observation in Eastern Turkey, VIII 7.

Palmer, Captain, H. M. S., III 5.

Wadhams, Commander A. V., V 12.

Wagner, General, Austrian officer, and drill-master in the Persian army, V 13.

Wilkes, Admiral, VII 21.

Wilson, Gen. James H., U. S. A., of the American forces in Peking, I 7.

2. AUTHORS, EDITORS, AND JOURNALISTS.

Advertiser, Boston Daily, IV 14.

Arnold, Sir Edwin, IV 9.

Bainbridge, W. F., Author, IV 10.

Barrett, Hon. James, Journalist, and U. S. Minister and Consul-General at Siam, I 12. VI 3.

Bishop, Mrs. Isabella Bird, Traveler, and Author, III 9. VIII 9.

Bryan, William Jennings, Journalist and Traveler, III 22.

Century, the Nineteenth, X 15.

Clemens, Samuel L., (Mark Twain), IV 3.

Clement, Ernest W., Newspaper Correspondent and Author, IV 6.

3. CHURCH OFFICIALS.

4. CIVIL OFFICERS AND DIPLOMATS.

AUTHORITIES CLASSIFIED

5. EDUCATORS.

AUTHORITIES CLASSIFIED

Moore, Prof. Edward C., Ph.D., D.D., Harvard University,
    I 11.
Peabody, Rev. Endicott, Headmaster Groton School, Massa-
    setts, VIII 6.
Silliman, Prof., Yale University, X 4.

6. NATIVES OF MISSION LANDS, OFFICIALS AND WRITERS

Avergal, Judge Varado Rao, B.A., B.L., Assistant Sessions
    Judge of Madura II 11.
Bharnajgree, Sir Muncherjee, a Parsee Member of Parlia-
    ment, VII 22.
Chang, Li Hung, China's greatest statesman, I 10.
Chulalongkorn, King of Siam, VII 24.
Damrong, Prince, Minister of the Interior for Siam, VII 7.
Fong, Tuan, Viceroy of Fukien, China, Special Commissioner
    to the United States, VII 30. X 25.
Fukuzawa, Mr., Editor of the Jiji Shimpo, Japan, IV 12.
Ito, Marquis, Prime Minister of Japan, VII 9.
Iyer, W. W. Subramania, Editor, II 12.
Japanese, a commanding officer, VII 17.
Japanese, a non-Christian, II 15.
Khan, Prince Malcolm, Persian Minister, X 12.
Korea, King of, VII 27.
Lewanika, King of the Barotsis, VII 15.
Maejima, Baron, Cabinet officer in Japan, VII 25.
Mukerji, Babu, Dakinaranjan, India, VIII 16.
Okuma, Count, Prime Minister, Japan, VII 14.
Pillai, Mr. Tirumalia, Special Deputy Collector, India,
    II 13.
Sen, Babu Keshub Chunder, X 23.
Shansi, Governor of, China, VII 4.
Singh, Kanwar, Sir Harnam, VIII 12.
Spectator, Indian, a non-Christian writer in, II 14.
Telang, Pweushotam Roa, a Brahmin, II 17.
Travancore, The Maharajah of, a native ruler, VII 2.
Yo, Ho, Chinese Consular General, IX 3.

THE MISSIONARY AND HIS CRITICS

7. SCIENTISTS AND PHYSICIANS.

Agassiz, Prof. Louis, VIII 8.

Cust, Dr. Robert N., IX 6.

Darwin, Charles, Naturalist, I 8. X 28.

Drummond, Henry, Scientist, Traveler, and Author, X 20.

Dudgeon, Dr. John, thirty years resident in China, head of
the Imperial College in Peking, Physician and Surgeon
of the British and Japanese Legations in Peking, V 7.

Kane, Dr., Arctic Explorer, X 11.

Meiniche, the Geographer, X 14.

Peters, Prof. John P., Ph.D., D.D., Sc.D., explorer and
author, VIII 25.

Ramsay, Prof. W. M., Archaeologist, III 17.

Schweinfurth, Dr., Scientist and Explorer, III 20.

Stanley, Sir Henry M., Explorer, III 10. VIII 10.

Wallace Alfred Russel, Scientist and Author, V 2.

8. UNCLASSIFIED.

Abbott, Edward, D.D., III 12. VI 11.

Arnold-Forster, Sir H. O., V 8.

Ball, J. Dyer, Esq., Hong Kong, X 19.

Barton, Miss Clara, President of American Red Cross Society,
III 13.

Bredon, Mr. R. E., IX 1.

Bronson, Rev. Dillon, III 15.

Cooper, Mr. H. Stonehewer, III 16.

Elliott, Sir Charles, X 24.

Muir, Sir W., X 3.

Nobleman, a, British, V 4.

Northbrook, the Earl of, VII 1.

Stevenson, William Fleming, X 8. 33.

COUNTRIES MENTIONED

III

AFRICA.

BULGARIA

THE MISSIONARY AND HIS CRITICS

COUNTRIES MENTIONED

Medhurst, Mr., British Consul at Shanghai, China, VI 10.

Michie, A., author of " Missionaries in China," IV 8.

Salisbury, Marquis of, Premier, England, VI 20.

Seward, Hon. George F., United States Minister to China, VI 6.

Shansi, Governor of, China, VII 4.

Stevenson, William Fleming, X 33.

Stratton, Hon. F. S., Collector of the Port of San Francisco, III 3.

Times, London, IV 4.

Ward, William Hayes, LL.D., Editor of the New York Independent, II 7.

Wilson, General James H., U. S. A. of the American forces in Peking, I 7.

Yo, Ho, Chinese Consular General, IX 3.

GREENLAND.

Kane, Dr., Arctic explorer, X 11.

HAWAII.

Adams, John Quincy, President of the United States, X 5.

Allen, Hon. Elisha H., Hawaiian Minister to the United States, X 31.

Childs, Archdeacon Thomas Spencer, V 5.

Dana, Hon. Richard H., X 21.

Hoar, Hon. George F., United States Senator from Massachusetts, IX 10.

Jones, Capt. Thomas Catesby, who negotiated and signed the first formal treaty between the Hawaiian Islands and the United States, VI 16.

Twain, Mark (Samuel L. Clemens), IV 3.

INDIA.

Abbott, Edward, D. D., III 12.

Aitchison, Sir C. U., Lieut. Governor of the Punjab, VII 3.

THE MISSIONARY AND HIS CRITICS

COUNTRIES MENTIONED

JAPAN.

THE MISSIONARY AND HIS CRITICS

Khan, Prince Malcolm, Persian Minister, X 12.
Wagner, Gen., Austrian officer, and drill-master in the Persian army, V 13.

SIAM.

Barrett, Hon. John, Journalist and United States Minister, and Consul-General at Siam, I 12. VI 3.
Belknap, Geo. E., Rear Admiral, United States Navy, X 18.
Chulalongkorn, King of Siam, VII 24.
Damrong, Prince, Minister of the Interior for Siam, VII 7.
King, Hon. Hamilton, United States Consul-General to Siam, VI 5.
Sickles, Hon. David B., United States Consul at Bangkok, Siam, VI 17.

SOUTH AMERICA.

Darwin, Charles, Naturalist, I 8.
Stevenson, William Fleming, X 33.

TURKEY.

Ambassador, an English, at Constantinople, VIII 5.
Angell, James B., LL.D., president of the University of Michigan, and formerly Minister to China and Turkey, IX 14. X 1.
Barton, Miss Clara, President of American Red Cross Society, III 13.
Baxter, William E., M.P., III 14.
Bryce, Hon. James, M.P., V 11. IX 5.
Currie, Sir Philip, British Ambassador to Constantinople, VIII 4.
Hepworth, George H., Editor and Author, IX 8.
Norton, Thomas H., Ph. D., United States Consul at Harpoot and Smyrna, Turkey, I 17. X 30.
Noyes, Hon. E. F., United States Minister to Turkey, VI 9.

IV

CONTRIBUTION OF MISSIONS.

1. To Commerce and Trade.

2. To Civilization.

3. To General Enlightenment.

CONTRIBUTION OF MISSIONS

4. To Good Government.

I	2.	VII	2, 12, 25, 26, 28.
V	8, 9, 11.	VIII	18, 20.
VI	15, 23.	IX	11.

5. To Science and Literature.

IV	1, 13, 15.	IX	3, 6.
VI	12.	X	4, 21, 22.
VIII	8, 14, 21, 23.		

6. To the Comfort of the People.

I	2, 13, 15.	VI	4, 5, 6.
II	4, 6, 7, 8, 12, 13.	VII	4, 15, 23.
III	2.	VIII	5.
IV	3, 7.	IX	13.
V	12, 14, 15.	X	10.